# Instant Expert: **World Religions**

17

# INSTANT EXPERT
# WORLD
# RELIGIONS

→ Joanne O'Brien and
Sandra Palmer

LION

Published by Lion Books
an imprint of
**Lion Hudson plc**
Wilkinson House, Jordan Hill Road,
Oxford OX2 8DR, England
www.lionhudson.com/lion

ISBN 978 0 7459 5576 6
e-ISBN 978 0 7459 5784 5

First edition 2013

**Acknowledgments**

Scripture quotations taken from the Holy Bible, New
International Version, copyright © 1973, 1978, 1984
International Bible Society. Used by permission of Hodder &
Stoughton, a member of the Hodder Headline Group. All rights
reserved. "NIV" is a trademark of International Bible Society.
UK trademark number 1448790.
The Apostle's Creed and the Lord's Prayer as they appear
in *Common Worship: Services and Prayers for the Church of
England* (Church House Publishing, 2000) are copyright © The
English Language Liturgical Consultation and are reproduced
by permission of the publisher.

A catalogue record for this book is available from the
British Library

Printed and bound in the UK, February 2013, LH26

# Contents

# Introduction

Over two-thirds of the world's peoples profess allegiance to a religion. This book is a snapshot of the beliefs and practices of eleven religions, although we recognize that for some adherents religion is a cultural identity rather than a way of life. As there are too many religions in the world to accommodate them all in a small book, we have chosen those with wide historical and religious significance, rather than using the number of followers as our sole criteria for inclusion.

In order to give a glimpse of the breadth and complexity of religions in a book of this length, we have chosen to write about some in greater depth than others. This decision does not reflect the impact or importance of the religions that we have written about more briefly.

Different religions have different ways of calculating and dating the year of an event. The designations BC ("before Christ") and AD (*Anno Domini*, "in the year of the Lord") reflect a Christian perspective, and we have decided to continue with these abbreviations, as they are widely used, rather than using BCE ("Before the Common Era") and CE ("Common Era").

# The Bahá'í Faith

Followers of the Bahá'í Faith, known as Bahá'ís, believe that God has been revealed at different times through different prophets. Each revelation was relevant to its particular place and time. For this present age God sent the prophet Mirza Husayn-'Ali Nuri, born in 1817, now known by his religious title of Bahá'u'lláh – "the Glory of God". As the world changes and progresses, Bahá'ís believe that all people should be united, not divided by nation, race, and religion.

There are around 5 million Bahá'ís in communities spread throughout the world. They are governed through local and national elected bodies called Spiritual Assemblies. They also have a world-governing council that is based at the Bahá'í World Centre in Haifa, Israel. This is called the Universal House of Justice.

## Beginnings

The Bahá'í Faith began in the middle of the nineteenth century in Iran (Persia) with the visionary dreams and subsequent teachings of Siyyid 'Ali-Muhammad Shirazi. He was born in 1819 into a Shia Muslim family.

As a young man Siyyid 'Ali-Muhammad felt that
the spirit of God had entered and inspired him and in
1844 announced that he was a "Báb" or "gate". In Shia
tradition this is a way in which God communicates
with humanity. His teachings attracted a wide circle of
followers, but his religious claims also brought strong
opposition. He was executed by firing squad in 1850.
Before his death, he declared that a new prophet
would arise – Bahá'ís believe that Bahá'u'lláh is this
new prophet.

Bahá'u'lláh followed the teachings of the Báb, which
led to his imprisonment in 1852. He had a series of
mystical visions in prison that revealed his divine
mission. In 1863 Bahá'u'lláh finally declared to his
close followers that he was the promised one – the
new prophet. He was exiled to the city of Acre in
present-day Israel where he continued to write and
teach. Bahá'u'lláh died in 1892 and appointed his son,
'Abdu'l-Bahá, as his successor.

## Scriptures

The writings of the Báb and Bahá'u'lláh are believed to
be divinely revealed. These form the scriptures along
with the writings and transcribed talks of 'Abdu'l-
Bahá. Many Bahá'ís also read the scriptures of other
faiths for religious enlightenment, but they are not
binding on Bahá'í belief and practice.

## Unity of all people

*"The earth is but one country and mankind its citizens."*
Bahá'u'lláh

Because of their belief in the unity of all people, Bahá'ís campaign to promote equality and economic justice. They also work towards providing equal access to education, regardless of class and race. Bahá'ís are often involved in grassroots initiatives in their home towns and villages as this is an expression of faith in action.

## Bahá'í prayer and worship

Bahá'ís meet informally at devotional meetings and study circles. These are an opportunity to pray, share spiritual experiences, and develop friendships in the local community.

The Bahá'í community has also built seven Houses of Worship, at least one on each continent. Although they have distinctive designs, they also have the unifying feature of nine sides and a central dome. The newest House of Worship, completed in 1986 in New Delhi, is the shape of a lotus flower. These places of worship are open to people of all religions, and there are no clergy or set rituals.

# Buddhism

Buddhism aims to help people find a way to let go of attachments that make them unhappy, such as fear, greed, or regret. It offers a path to understand the cause of suffering and to find release from it. Through careful reflection people can have a clearer view of why they feel, act, and react in the way they do – they start to understand the effects of their feelings and actions.

In order to find happiness, Buddhism teaches that it is necessary for people to look first within themselves. With guidance, practice, and knowledge, this leads to increased kindness and compassion to all living things and, in turn, to increased wisdom. Buddhists believe in an endless cycle of death and rebirth, and the final aim of the Buddhist path is for individuals to break the ties of rebirth and find release from suffering.

## Beginnings

Siddhartha Gautama, who was born in northern India around the end of the sixth century BC, sought an answer to the cause of suffering and the path to liberation from it.

According to tradition, he was born into a wealthy family and protected from the hardships and realities of everyday life, but he began to think about life beyond his privileged background. One story tells how he asked his father's charioteer to take him to the nearby city. On the journey he witnessed sickness, ageing, and death for the first time. He also saw the inner calm of a wandering ascetic, a man who had renounced earthly belongings to follow a religious and spiritual quest.

Deeply affected by what he had seen and disillusioned with his wealthy life, he left home and became an ascetic, seeking to understand the nature and cause of suffering and death. According to traditional reckoning, he was twenty-nine years of age. He studied with various teachers, and at one stage he practised extreme austerities – for six years he ate and drank just enough to stay alive – but he still could not find the answer.

Finally, Siddhartha realized the truth did not lie in extremes but in the Middle Way. While sitting in meditation under a tree, he understood the cause and nature of suffering and the path to find release from it. Siddhartha became Buddha – this means "the Awakened One" or "the Enlightened One".

## The Buddha's first teachings

After his enlightenment the Buddha gave his first sermon in a deer park at Sarnath. Here he taught the Four Noble Truths and said the mind must first be at peace in order to understand them:

- The first Noble Truth: suffering exists.

- The second Noble Truth: there is a cause of suffering.
- The third Noble Truth: there is a way to end suffering.
- The fourth Noble Truth: the way to end suffering is through the Eightfold Path.

The Eightfold Path is called the Middle Way – it is the path that the Buddha himself experienced. Buddhists look for a teacher to guide them as the path requires concentration and discipline:

right opinion
right thoughts
right speech
right action
right livelihood
right effort
right mindfulness
right concentration.

## The first monks and nuns

The Buddha travelled and taught across northeastern India for forty-five years, gathering followers who embraced his teachings. These early disciples formed the first community of monks and nuns, the *Sangha*. The code of conduct or discipline that the Buddha laid down for the *Sangha* is called the *Vinaya*. This code still guides their behaviour, provides training for their spiritual life, helps maintain monastic unity, and ensures harmony with the wider community.

## A robe and alms bowl

Monks and nuns follow the Buddha's example by owning the most basic necessities including a robe and an alms bowl to accept food offered by the lay community. Members of the *Sangha* do not beg; they are given offerings and in return provide the precious gift of the Buddha's teachings.

Buddhist robes are designed to meet the essential needs of covering the body to protect it from heat or cold and to ward off insects. The colour and style also reflect the culture and climate in which they are worn. In the Buddha's time the robes of ascetics were made of discarded pieces of cloth or clothing that were sewn together and coloured using natural vegetable dyes, resulting in a variety of earth tones.

### Buddhist monasteries

Buddhist monasteries are called *viharas*. This name originally referred to the secluded places where early Buddhist monks and nuns sought refuge during the rainy season.

Monks do not leave their monasteries during the three months of the rainy season in Thailand, Cambodia, Burma, Laos, and Sri Lanka. This rainy period is also the traditional time for boys and young men to become temporary novices in a monastery.

## Development of Buddhism

In the centuries following the Buddha's death different viewpoints appeared in the interpretation of his teachings. By the first century AD two forms of Buddhism emerged: Theravada and Mahayana.

### Theravada Buddhism

This is the name given to the tradition that most closely follows the teachings and traditions established during the time of the Buddha and in the following centuries. It means "Teachings of the Elders".

Theravada Buddhism, sometimes called "Southern Buddhism", is mainly practised in Thailand, Cambodia, Burma, Laos, and Sri Lanka.

### Mahayana Buddhism

During the first century AD as the teachings developed and spread, a form of Buddhism called Mahayana emerged. It means "Great Vehicle". In the Mahayana tradition there is a belief in *bodhisattvas* – beings who are on the path to becoming Buddha, but have chosen to delay their final release from rebirth out of compassion to help all creatures.

Mahayana Buddhism that is practised in China, Japan, Korea, and Vietnam is often called "Eastern Buddhism". Mahayana Buddhism that is mainly practised in Tibet, Mongolia, Bhutan, parts of China, and the Himalayan regions of Nepal and India is often called "Northern Buddhism".

Over 98 per cent of the world's Buddhists live in Asia, and Buddhism is the religion of the majority in Thailand, Cambodia, Burma, Laos, Sri Lanka, and the Himalayan kingdom of Bhutan. Following the political freedoms of the 1990s, Buddhism is once again the major religion in Mongolia. Buddhism has also grown considerably in the West, and there are more than 3 million Buddhists in the USA, over 1.5 million in Europe, and around 700,000 in Latin America.

## The Dalai Lama

The Dalai Lama is the spiritual leader of Tibetan Buddhism. He is believed to be a living manifestation of the Bodhissatva of Compassion, Avalokiteshvara, and is fourteenth in the line of reincarnated Dalai Lamas.

Between 1950 and 1951 China invaded Tibet, and in 1959 the Dalai Lama fled to India after the suppression of a national uprising. The Dalai Lama's Tibetan government-in-exile is based at Dharamsala in northern India. Here there are approximately 18,500 Tibetan monks and nuns and many thousands of Tibetan refugees.

## Buddhist beliefs

The Buddha taught that attachment keeps individuals tied to rebirth, to the cycle of suffering. This may be caused by greed or delusion, trying to hold on to happiness or regret, or jealousy of other people or belongings. The Buddha said his teachings are like a raft that helps people cross from ignorance to knowledge. As desire and confusion fade, inner wisdom grows. When an individual fully understands the illusionary nature of all things, they no longer have a sense of self that keeps them attached to thoughts or emotions. Their desires will be extinguished and they will find release from suffering.

The historical Buddha taught that there have been Buddhas in the past and there will be others in the future, but they are rare and extraordinary beings. Buddhas embody perfect wisdom; they teach out of compassion for the suffering of others, so that others may also find enlightenment.

## Samsara

*Samsara* means "wandering" – the endless cycle of rebirth. Beings wander through the vast universe searching for happiness and security, being reborn in different forms. The Buddha said this wandering has been going on for aeons and will continue for aeons in the future. The path that he taught offers release from it. The state beyond rebirth is called *nirvana*, the extinguishing of all desires and suffering. Although words cannot fully encompass this state, it is sometimes described as supreme peace and happiness.

*Karma*

*Karma* means "action" or "deed". Buddhists believe
that the actions we choose produce results in this life
or future lives. The Buddha said humans are tied to
*karma* just as a wheel is attached to a cart by an axle.
Intentional actions affect *karma*, so if an individual's
thinking is confused, their actions are confused.
However, meditation develops clarity of thinking and
self-awareness. An intentional action might set in
motion an unpleasant outcome, but a positive action
can influence the final result. For example, the pain
created by an angry outburst might be eased through
a truthful apology.

All things are subject to the law of *karma*, and with
skilful practice it is possible to generate positive
*karma*. The final aim is to break free from karmic ties –
when craving and attachment cease, the sense of self
ceases so there is nothing to be reborn.

The Buddha said, "Whoever sees the *Dharma*, sees
me. Whoever sees me, sees *Dharma*." The *Dharma* is
the Buddha's teachings and the path of practice that
leads to knowledge and understanding. The *Dharma*
also refers to the true nature and order of all things.

The Buddha, the *Dharma* and the *Sangha* are
called the "Three Jewels". Before offering devotion,
Buddhists bow three times and repeat:

*I take refuge in the Buddha,*
*I take refuge in the Dharma,*
*I take refuge in the Sangha.*

This is a traditional expression of trust and confidence – a commitment to the Buddhist path.

## Buddhist scriptures

The Buddha said that his words would become the teacher. Theravada and Mahayana traditions both record the Buddha's teachings and conversations, but Mahayana texts also contain the writing of sages and scholars, new words attributed to the Buddha, and commentaries on them.

### *Theravada scriptures*

These are written in Pali (the Buddha spoke a dialect of Pali). Initially handed down orally by monks and nuns, the scriptures were recorded on palm leaves in the first century BC in Sri Lanka and form the Pali Canon. The collection is divided into three parts, called the *Tripitaka* or "Three Baskets", recalling the baskets in which the scriptures were originally stored. They are:

- *Sutta* – the Buddha's teachings
- *Vinaya* – the rules of conduct
- *Abhidhamma* – "higher teachings" and accompanying commentaries.

### *Mahayana scriptures*

The earliest were written in Sanskrit, the common sacred language of ancient India, in the first century AD.

As Buddhism spread and developed, scriptures were translated and new ones added. The two main sources for Mahayana scriptures are the collections of texts from China and Tibet.

- Chinese scriptures: Known as the "Great Scripture Store", it consists of over 2,000 texts. It is also used in the Korean and Japanese Buddhist traditions, although there is some difference in the arrangement and contents of these canons of literature.

- Tibetan scriptures: Divided into two collections, these are "Translations of the Word of the Buddha" and "Translations of Treatises", which include commentaries on the Buddha's teachings in addition to poetry and hymns.

## Buddhist practice

In order to reduce selfishness and act with compassion, Buddhists try to be aware of their actions and the effect they have. They are following step seven of the Eightfold Path – they are practising mindfulness. Mindful actions lead to generosity, which loosens attachment to material belongings – it helps free the mind from selfish acts. Giving, or *dana*, leads to good conduct, which helps develop more skilled states of meditation. These more refined states of mind help Buddhists practise the Five Precepts, the basics of Buddhist ethics and morality.

*The Five Precepts*

The precepts are practical training for spiritual development – they help to develop individual clarity of mind and respect for others. During periods of monastic retreat or on festival days, lay Buddhists sometimes observe eight precepts and monks observe the precepts in their strictest form. By following the ethics of the Five Precepts, Buddhists undertake to refrain from the following:

- Harming living beings: encourages loving-kindness

- Taking what is not given: encourages right livelihood and generosity

- Sexual misconduct: promotes self-restraint and mutual trust

- False speech: encourages integrity and respect for truth

- Clouding the mind with alcohol or drugs: avoids loss of self-control, which can lead to breaking the other four precepts.

*Meditation*

Meditation is a way of clearing the mind – of freeing it from hindrances that cloud the senses. There are two types of meditation: *samatha* and *vipassana*. *Samatha* calms the mind by focusing it totally on an object or a sensation, such as the rise and fall of breathing or the flickering of a flame. This lays the foundation for *vipassana*, which develops insight into the sense of self, the cause of suffering, and the path to end it.

## Chanting

In monasteries and temples, or alone in front of a shrine, the deep rhythmic sound of chanting is a way to focus the mind and create feelings of joy and peace. Chanting *sutras* or *mantras* from Buddhist scriptures is used in meditation practice, in personal devotion, and for reflection or study. Chanting also plays a prominent role in ceremonies and festivals.

In the Theravada tradition, monks also perform protective chanting to ward off sickness, bring blessings, or protect from danger – this chanting is called *paritta*. In the Tibetan tradition, the mantra *Om Mane Padme Hum* is frequently chanted silently or aloud. It calls upon the Bodhisattva of Compassion, Avalokiteshvara, and is said to be the essence of all the Buddha's teachings.

Death is the most important rite of passage within Buddhism. Buddhists hope to die in a calm state of mind, free of regrets, and monks are often invited to chant during the final hours of life and at funerals. In the Tibetan tradition, readings are said for the dying from the Tibetan *Book of the Dead*; this is believed to guide the dead on their forty-nine day journey from one life to the next.

### *Sutras* and mantras

*Sutras,* or *suttas* in the Pali language, are the discourses or teachings attributed to the Buddha. Sutra means "thread" in Sanskrit and conveys the idea of material being drawn together. It is thought another meaning might be "something that is well said" from the Sanskrit word sukta.

Mantras are a sequence of syllables or words believed to embody spiritual power; they may also have healing or protective qualities. They are chanted repeatedly to direct the mind towards clarity and wisdom.

## Buddhist festivals

Festivals generally follow the lunar calendar and vary according to the Southern, Eastern, and Northern traditions. Festivals might be local to an area or temple while others are nationally celebrated. All Buddhists celebrate the Buddha's birth, enlightenment, and passing into *nirvana*. All three events are celebrated on the same day at the festival of Vesakha in Southern Buddhism, and at the festival of Saka Dawa in Northern Buddhism. It is a day of devotion and increased religious observance. The lights and lanterns that decorate temples and houses symbolize the light of the Buddha's awakening. In Eastern Buddhism, these events in the Buddha's life are celebrated at separate festivals.

The female form of the *bodhisattva* Avalokiteshvara is Guan Yin – the "regarder of cries". Out of great compassion she is believed to hear the calls of those who suffer and need protection or guidance. In Eastern Buddhism Guan Yin's birthday, enlightenment, and becoming *bodhisattva* are celebrated in the second, sixth, and ninth lunar months respectively.

## New Year
New Year is widely celebrated in all Buddhist traditions as homes are cleaned to sweep away negative aspects of the previous year, special food is prepared, and devotions are offered at home shrines and in temples. In Japan, crowds flock to temples for their first visit of the year, many arriving before the sun has risen. In Thailand, statues of the Buddha are ritually washed, and crowds throng the streets for boisterous water festivals that mark a time of renewal. In Tibet, New Year festivities continue through the first lunar month, and in Lhasa they culminate with Monlam Chemno, the Great Prayer Festival.

## Guru Rinpoche's birthday
Guru Rinpoche, or "Precious Teacher", is the title given to the Indian teacher Padmasambhava who established Buddhism in Tibet in the eighth century AD. His birthday is celebrated on the tenth day of the sixth lunar month in the Northern Buddhist calendar. Temple visits are made to hear chanting and sermons from the monks, and celebrations continue with feasts, dancing, and storytelling.

*Ullambana*

*Ullambana* means "to hang upside down" and implies deep suffering. Falling on the fifteenth day of the seventh lunar month, this festival honours the ancestors and calms unsettled spirits, helping to deliver them from suffering. Merit is transferred to the deceased through the chanting of monks, devotional offerings, and acts of charity. In Japan it is celebrated in mid July and called O Bon, a time for families to clean graves, offer incense, and light lanterns to guide the spirits of the dead safely back. Fires are also lit at home to welcome returning spirits and to bid them farewell at the close of the festival.

In China this time is called the Hungry Ghosts festival and focuses on placating the spirits of the dead who did not receive proper burial rites and are free to roam the world at this time.

## Buddhist pilgrimage

Buddhist scriptures mention four places associated with the Buddha that should be visited with feelings of reverence – they are the sites of the Buddha's birth, enlightenment, first sermon, and *parinirvana* – his final passing into *nirvana*.

The Buddha recommended that faithful monks, nuns, and lay people visit these sites, and they remain important destinations for Buddhists from all traditions.

- Lumbini – the Buddha was born in a grove of trees at Lumbini, which is now is south-west Nepal.

- Bodh Gaya – the Buddha realized enlightenment under a pipal tree, which came to be known as the "Bodhi" or "Enlightenment" tree. Bodh Gaya is south of the city of Patna.

- Sarnath – the Buddha gave his first sermon to a group of five disciples in a deer park at Sarnath, close to the city of Varanasi.

- Kusinagara – the Buddha died on a simple bed beneath two sala trees at Kusinagara, which is in the state of Uttar Pradesh.

There are also many other pilgrimage sites, including Siripada in Sri Lanka, the mountain on which the Buddha is said to have left his footprints, Mount Kailas in Tibet, and four sacred Buddhist mountains in China, each one associated with a *bodhisattva*. Pilgrimages are an act of devotion and commitment and a way to generate positive *karma*. Pilgrims may be inspired by the people and teachings associated with a certain place, by the feelings of peace or happiness they experience, and by the positive effect it has on their thoughts and actions.

### Stupas

*Stupa* comes from a Sanskrit word meaning "to heap" or "to pile up". The first stupas were built to cover the relics of the Buddha. They were simple clay or mud-brick mounds and were early sites of pilgrimage. Over time, stupas became more elaborate and evolved according to the architectural styles of different countries – for example, pagodas in China, chortens in Tibet, and dagobas in Sri Lanka. As well as relics linked to the Buddha, stupas also hold scriptures, relics of enlightened teachers and monks, and objects belonging to them such as robes or alms bowls.

# Christianity

Christianity teaches that God is ultimately beyond human comprehension but has chosen to reveal his nature through his son – Jesus Christ – and that because of Jesus it is possible to have a relationship with God.

## Beginnings

Christianity began in the first century AD in Palestine, now Israel, at a time when it was ruled by the Romans. The followers of Jesus, an itinerant preacher from Nazareth, believed that he had risen from the dead, having been crucified on the orders of Pontius Pilate, the Roman governor. They spread the teachings of Jesus, and the hope of resurrection and a new life in which love overcomes hatred, despair, and death. The first Christians met with persecution until the Emperor Constantine converted to Christianity in the fourth century AD.

Little is known of Jesus before the age of thirty, when he began to travel the countryside with twelve disciples. According to four accounts of his life, the Gospels, he healed the sick, performed other miracles, and preached using sayings and stories called parables. The essence of his teaching was that

God is love and loves everyone, especially those who are rejected by society. He taught that God's kingdom would come very soon.

Jesus was a Jew and known as a rabbi, or teacher. He taught a radical form of Judaism that emphasized the spirit rather than letter of the Law, which Jews believed God gave to their ancestor Moses. This brought him into conflict with other Jewish groups – rabbis known as the Pharisees, and the Sadducees, who were based in the Temple in Jerusalem. The first Christians were also Jews and believed Jesus to be the fulfilment of Jewish prophecies. This is why they continued to regard the Jewish scriptures as God's word; they are now known as the Old Testament.

The word *Christ* means "messiah" or "saviour anointed of God". There was an ancient belief in Israel that God would send someone as a messiah to save the people from their enemies and bring a reign of peace. Jesus' followers believed that he was this messiah and so he became known as "Jesus Christ", and they became known as "Christians". Very early on they believed that Jesus brought spiritual rather than political salvation.

## Developments and divisions

There were two main centres of Christianity in the first millennium AD – the Western Church based in Rome and the Eastern Church based in Constantinople (now Istanbul). There were also Christian communities as far away as India and

China, as well as around the Mediterranean. In the eleventh century an argument about the wording of the Nicene Creed – a statement of faith – led to a split between the two: the Western Church became known as the Catholic Church, and the Eastern Church was known as the Orthodox Church.

Protestant Christianity sprang from reform movements in Europe in the sixteenth century and rebellions against the teachings and practices of the Roman Church. For the Protestant reformers, such as Martin Luther in Germany, it was faith in God's love that brought salvation, not obedience to the church or the keeping of rules. Since those early days the Protestant movement has fractured into over 33,000 denominations, if very small independent churches are included.

Emigration and a strong sense of mission have taken Christianity all over the world so that there are now over 2 billion Christians. Nearly half are Roman Catholics, but Protestant churches, especially in the developing world, are the most rapidly growing.

*The Orthodox, Catholic, and Protestant traditions*
Orthodox and Catholic churches have a strong liturgical tradition, with worship in a set order, set prayers, and rituals that draw on all the senses. Priests wear robes in liturgical colours and there is often incense. Their buildings, whether a grand cathedral, a parish church, or a small chapel, have statues and images. In the Orthodox tradition these images are

icons painted according to strict guidelines and many are on a screen, the iconostasis, which divides the congregation from the area of the altar.

Both churches have priesthoods – only the priests may perform certain rituals for them to be valid. They both have hierarchies – from archbishop or patriarch, to bishop, to priest. Only a bishop may ordain a priest. Roman Catholic priests are not married, except for a few who were priests in the Anglican church first. Orthodox priests may marry but a bishop must be celibate.

The Orthodox and Catholic traditions are both sacramental forms of Christianity. It is believed that God's grace is given and experienced through the observance of sacraments – though what counts as a sacrament and the exact number differ. They include baptism, Eucharist (breaking of bread), marriage, anointing the sick, confirmation, and confession. The consecration of the bread and wine takes place at the altar.

Mary, the mother of Jesus, is honoured in both Orthodox and Catholic churches as the mother of God, since Jesus is believed to be God.

Protestant churches often have ministers or pastors instead of priests, and many have a strong egalitarian tradition. They tend to emphasize the authority of the Bible and personal conversion over the authority of the church and sacraments. Communal worship is often informal, and at least partly extempore rather than following a written order of service. The Lord's table is used instead of an altar. Some Protestant groups do not have purpose-built churches but meet instead in schools or other suitable buildings.

Music is widely used in Christian worship. Some is ancient, going back centuries, and some is very modern.

All Christians use the cross as a symbol. Protestant churches usually have a simple bare cross; Catholics and Orthodox often have crucifixes with the figure of Jesus on the cross.

### The term "Catholic"

The word "catholic" is used in three ways. With a small "c" it refers to the whole universal church. With a capital "C" it refers to a sacramental liturgical tradition that includes a stream within the Church of England. The Roman Catholic church refers to the worldwide church based in Rome with the pope as its head and authority on earth.

## Christian scriptures

The Bible is believed to be the word of God. It is a collection of sixty-six books written over a period of between 500 and a thousand years and is divided into two parts – the Old and New Testaments. It contains a variety of genres: myth, history, laws, poetry, prophecies, and letters. The New Testament contains the Gospels (Matthew, Mark, Luke, and John), an account of the early church (the Acts of the Apostles), and letters written by early church leaders, including the apostle Paul. Most of the Old Testament was written in Hebrew. The New Testament was written in Greek because that was the language widely read through the Mediterranean world, though Jesus spoke Aramaic. The complete Bible has been translated into over 400 languages, and the New Testament into over a thousand.

Some Christians take the Bible literally and believe that as the word of God it must be true in every detail. Others think that it reflects the worldviews of the periods in which it was written and believe that while some parts are myth and legend, it is true in its teachings about the nature of God, God's relationship with all creation, and the purpose and meaning of life.

It is Orthodox and Roman Catholic teaching that the Bible must be understood and interpreted under the guidance of the church. Protestants read the Bible directly for themselves, though in practice there are strong traditions of interpretations within Protestant communities.

Some copies of the Bible are treated with reverence, especially those used in worship in Orthodox and Catholic churches. Christians often have their own copies that they use for study. There are no special rules for the care of personal Bibles – some Christians make notes in the margins as they study.

## Dating the New Testament

Letters by the Christian missionary Paul are the earliest books of the New Testament, thought to be written from around AD 50 to 68. The Gospels of Matthew, Mark, and Luke have so much overlapping material that most scholars think that the authors of Matthew and Luke used the Gospel of Mark and another common source to write their Gospels. These are known as the "synoptic gospels". The earliest Gospel is thought to be Mark's, written around AD 65 to 70, although this is much debated.

The canon, the final closed list of writings to be included in the Bible, was settled by the beginning of the fifth century AD, though there are minor differences between denominations.

## Beliefs

Christianity is a monotheistic religion, teaching that there is one all-powerful, all-loving, providential God who created heaven and earth and revealed himself in his son Jesus to save the world.

### The Trinity

Christians believe God is one being in three persons: God, the creator and transcendent father; God the son; and God the Holy Spirit. This is known as the Trinity. The creeds teach that Jesus is God incarnate. Many rites, including baptism, finish with the statement, "in the name of the Father, Son and Holy Spirit". Acceptance of the doctrine of the Trinity is a requirement for membership of the World Council of Churches, a worldwide fellowship of 349 churches seeking unity, a common witness, and Christian service.

## Original sin

Since Bishop Augustine of Hippo in the fifth century AD, the Western Church has taught that all are born into original sin, bearing the sin of Adam and Eve who disobeyed God by taking the forbidden fruit from the tree in the Garden of Eden. This original sin is forgiven at baptism (Catholic tradition) or on acceptance of Jesus as a personal saviour (Protestant tradition).

A liberal interpretation of the doctrine is that everyone makes mistakes as part of learning, and that all are accepted and loved by God.

## Salvation: forgiveness of sins

The life, death, and resurrection of Jesus are believed to heal the relationship between humanity and God, between the individual and God. Jesus brings true living in this life and eternal salvation in the world to come. This is understood in different ways, including:

- **Victory:** the resurrection demonstrates that God is victorious over sin, death, and the devil.

- **Sacrifice:** Jesus offered himself as a sacrifice for humanity in order to pay a debt owed to God. Humans owe God a debt of obedience because he made them. Only a person without sin can pay this debt. Jesus was the only one without sin and was obedient to God until death. His sacrifice paid the debt. Jesus bore the ultimate punishment – death on the cross – so that others can receive forgiveness.

- **Sharing**: God demonstrated his love for humanity by being willing to share fully in the human condition, even to the point of death as a common criminal.

## The life in the world to come

The resurrection of Jesus is a portent of the resurrection of all to come. Christians teach this world will end and there will be a new heaven and a new earth after a Day of Judgment. The last book of the Bible, the book of Revelation, paints a vivid picture of the last days. Some Christians take this literally, teaching a variety of versions of millennialism in which it is believed that the anti-Christ will rule for a thousand years before the end of time. Some scholars interpret the book of Revelation as a metaphorical account of the Roman empire of the time.

## Angels and devils

In the Bible angels are messengers of God. Many Christians also believe in a devil whom they identify with the serpent in the garden of Eden, the fallen angel Lucifer in the book of Isaiah, and Satan in the New Testament.

## The Creeds

Core Christian teachings are in two Christian statements of faith still said in many churches today. The longer of the two, the Nicene Creed, was the result of fifty years of debate begun in AD 325 at Nicea, Turkey, at a council of bishops convened by the emperor Constantine. The shorter Apostle's Creed was developed between the third and ninth centuries AD.

### The Apostle's Creed

*I believe in God, the Father almighty,*
*creator of heaven and earth.*

*I believe in Jesus Christ, his only Son, our Lord,*
*who was conceived by the Holy Spirit,*
*born of the Virgin Mary,*
*suffered under Pontius Pilate,*
*was crucified, died, and was buried;*
*he descended to the dead.*
*On the third day he rose again;*
*he ascended into heaven,*
*he is seated at the right hand of the Father,*
*and he will come to judge the living and the dead.*

*I believe in the Holy Spirit,*
*the holy catholic Church,*
*the communion of saints,*
*the forgiveness of sins,*
*the resurrection of the body,*
*and the life everlasting.*
*Amen.*

## The Holy Spirit

It is believed that God's spirit, the Holy Spirit, is given at chrismation (Orthodox tradition), confirmation (Catholic tradition), or conversion. Christians seek the guidance of the Holy Spirit and some believe that the Holy Spirit fills them with prayer, with words they don't always understand, as the Holy Spirit filled the disciples, causing them to speak in foreign tongues on the day of Pentecost. Such Christians are known as charismatics and may be Protestant or Catholic.

## Christian practice

At the heart of Christian living lies prayer. Christians pray to share their thoughts and worries with God, to seek guidance, to petition, to confess and ask forgiveness, to praise, give thanks, and give blessings. Some prayers are private and personal, and some follow the words of others. Many Christians meet specifically for prayer. Orthodox and Catholic Christians often use aids to prayer such as prayer beads and candles.

Saying a prayer for penance and confession is understood as a necessary preparation for partaking in communion, or the Eucharist. In Orthodox and Catholic traditions confession may be made to a priest.

**The Lord's Prayer**
This prayer dates back to Jesus and is widely said in private and public prayer:

*Our Father, who art in heaven,*
*hallowed be thy name;*
*thy kingdom come;*
*thy will be done;*
*on earth as it is in heaven.*
*Give us this day our daily bread.*
*And forgive us our trespasses,*
*as we forgive those who trespass against us.*
*And lead us not into temptation;*
*but deliver us from evil.*
*Amen.*

## Communal worship

Christians may meet during the week but the main service is usually on a Sunday, because Sunday is believed to be the day of Christ's resurrection. Some services may simply be hymns, prayers, and perhaps a sermon where the preacher gives a message or speaks about the Bible reading for the day.

Most Christians have a service based on sharing bread and wine, recalling how Jesus broke bread with his disciples at his last meal with them. How frequently this is held, the detail of the ceremony, and what is signified varies. According to Orthodox and Catholic traditions, the bread and the wine become the body and blood of Christ. It is through partaking in the sacraments that the gift of salvation is experienced. In Protestant denominations, sharing the bread and wine is an act of remembrance. The service is known variously as the mass, the Eucharist, communion, and the breaking of the bread.

## Monks and nuns

Some Orthodox and Catholic Christians feel the call to commit themselves to a celibate simple life, usually in community with others in monasteries (men) or convents (women). Some live alone or in a house with only a few others though their commitment is to the overarching Order to which they belong. They make vows of chastity, obedience and poverty. Many wear simple clothes called habits – these identify them as part of a Religious Order.

## Ethics

Christians often speak of living life in imitation of Christ, following his teachings and example.

The ethics of Jesus were based on love and the belief that God's kingdom was for everyone, not just a chosen people. Jesus said, "Love your neighbour as yourself" (see, for example, Matthew 22:39) and "Do to others as you would have them do to you"

(Luke 6:31); the neighbour included the enemy. Jesus deplored hypocrisy and was critical of those who self-righteously kept the Law but did not care for those around them, and who expected forgiveness but did not forgive others. He taught that forgiveness of others was core to being forgiven by God. The early church continued his themes. Paul wrote in his letter to the Galatians that the fruit of the spirit is love, joy, peace, longsuffering, gentleness, goodness, faith, meekness, and temperance. Hospitality was also important in the early Christian community.

Many Christians take the Bible as a source book for Christian moral rules and judgments. Key texts are the Ten Commandments found in the Old Testament, the teachings of Jesus in the Sermon on the Mount (see Matthew 5–7), and the writings of Paul. Other rules are deduced by extension; for example, some Christians see abortion as a form of murder. Differences in interpreting the Bible have led to some differences between Christians in moral judgments, especially in the areas of warfare, sexual morality, and the accumulation of wealth.

Some Christian moral philosophers emphasize the development of Christian character through the acquisition of virtues such as those described by Paul rather than strict adherence to rules. Giving to charity is also regarded as a virtue. These virtues are sometimes contrasted with vices such as gluttony, greed, and anger.

Liberation movements within the church build on the radical positions regarding social justice found in the Bible – that is, justice for the poor, dispossessed, and the marginalized.

## Christian festivals

All Christians observe Christmas and Easter as major festivals. Orthodox and Catholic Christians celebrate with full liturgies and exuberance that follow the mood of the festivals. The dates of these festivals usually differ according to the calendar used – Julian or Gregorian. Protestants tend to observe festivals more simply, with fewer rituals. Different countries have different foods and customs associated with each festival.

Orthodox and Catholic Christians also celebrate days associated with Mary, the mother of Jesus, and with saints, especially the saints associated with their church or their own name. Although in a broad sense a saint can refer to any holy or virtuous person, in these traditions the term refers to someone given special status due to the devout life they lived.

### *Lent and Easter*

This is the most important time in the religious calendar: the time when Christians remember Jesus' final days and celebrate his triumphal, joyful resurrection on Easter Sunday. The exact date of Easter varies yearly according to the phases of the moon. As it was developed first in the northern hemisphere, many of its rituals are associated with the coming of spring.

Lent is a period of reflection and abstinence beginning on Ash Wednesday and finishing on Maundy Thursday. The final days of Lent overlap with Holy Week, when Christians remember the last week of Jesus' life on earth. This consists of:

- Palm Sunday – which recalls Jesus being welcomed by the crowd, who waved palm leaves as he rode into Jerusalem on a donkey

- Maundy Thursday – which remembers Jesus' last supper with his disciples

- Good Friday – the day of Jesus' crucifixion.

Observing the events of Holy Week leads to the celebration of Easter Sunday.

## Advent and Christmas

Advent is a period of reflection, when Christians prepare for the coming birth of Jesus at Christmas and the return of Jesus on the Day of Judgment. Christmas is the celebration of Jesus' birth in a stable, because there was no room for his mother, Mary, to give birth in an inn. Epiphany, meaning "the divine revealed", recalls the wise men visiting Jesus twelve days after his birth. Gifts are given; children traditionally receive them from a secret magical person such as Father Christmas. Who that person is and which day in the season gifts are given varies between countries. Gift-giving symbolizes the gift of God's Son and recalls the gifts brought to the baby.

### Jesus' birthday

The exact date of Jesus' birth is unknown. Most Christians were observing 25 December by the fourth century AD for theological rather than historical reasons.

The year of Jesus' birth was assigned in the sixth century by Dionysius Exiguus, a scholar and abbot in Rome. This began a new practice of dating the year from the year of our Lord (*Anno Domini* – AD). Modern historians argue for a year between 8 and 4 BC as the year of Jesus' birth.

## Rites of passage

Christian life begins either with baptism or conversion. The ritual follows the example of Jesus who was baptized by his cousin John at the start of his ministry.

### Baptism

Many denominations baptize babies and infants, incorporating them into the church in the name of the Trinity – the Father, Son, and Holy Spirit. This may be by full immersion in water or by pouring water on the forehead. Godparents and parents make vows on behalf of babies who can later confirm those vows for themselves at confirmation. Some denominations only baptize those who can confirm their beliefs for themselves, and have dedication services for infants instead. For them baptism is an outward sign of an earlier commitment.

Baptism can take place at any time in life. In the first century AD Christians were often baptized close to death.

## Marriage

In Christian marriage God is both witness to and creator of the marriage. In most denominations the couple makes their vows of love and faithfulness until death in front of the officiant – a priest or minister – and at least two adults. Marriage is a gift and blessing for the couple and the wider community. Roman Catholics do not allow divorce since they believe that what God has made cannot be broken. Instead a marriage may be dissolved on the grounds that it was not a valid marriage in the first place. Other denominations permit divorce but dislike it and encourage taking marriage vows very seriously. Many Christians follow a teaching that the man is the head of the woman, and that men and women have different roles; others teach that God has created man and woman equal in all things.

## Death

Christian funerals commit the deceased to God in the hope of resurrection to a life with God in heaven. Sometimes priests are called to the dying to anoint them and say prayers, or the Last Rites, to give them spiritual strength for the journey to come.

# Pilgrimage

Many Christians make pilgrimages to holy places either alone or in groups. They are made for different purposes – for study or meditation, in thanksgiving, in penance, for healing, or to grant a particular prayer. Some places of pilgrimage are internationally known; others are more local, such as holy wells or shrines.

Popular places of pilgrimage include:

- Jerusalem and Israel – its association with Jesus brings Orthodox, Catholic, and Protestant pilgrims.

- Places associated with the apostle Paul, such as Rome, Corinth, and Thessalonica. Many church groups take tours to follow in the footsteps of Paul.

- Lourdes – a place of healing after an apparition of the Virgin Mary appeared to a village girl, Bernadette.

- Rome and the Vatican – the seat of the pope and a place of Roman Catholic pilgrimage.

- Santiago de Compostela – the walk is more important than the arrival at the church of St James in Santiago, Spain. Pilgrims start their walk in other countries in Europe, often walking the hundreds of miles alone and staying at simple shelters en route.

- Taize – an ecumenical community of Catholic and Protestant monks in France, which draws thousands of young Christians each year.

# Daoism

Daoism is a philosophical and religious tradition that originated in China and is followed by millions of people in China and beyond. The Dao is the way of nature, and Daoists try to live in harmony with its flow. *Dao* means "the Way" or "the Path". It is mysterious and infinite, producing all life and sustaining all things. Each individual needs to understand the nature of the Dao so that, instead of fighting against the flow of life, they become part of its rhythm and balance – they personally experience the Dao. Traditional Daoism is also rich in rituals, traditions, festivals, and mythology, and there is an extensive pantheon of deities who are honoured in shrines and temples.

The *Dao De Jing*, a classic Chinese text attributed to the sage Laozi, is a guide to living the way of the Dao. Laozi means "Old Master".

## Beginnings

Daoism grew out of the shamanic tradition that recognized physical and spiritual worlds alongside each other. After entering a trance, the shaman can travel between these two worlds, communicating with spirits to restore balance or bring healing. Shamans became the early "priests" of Daoism, performing rituals, reading oracles, and interpreting divinations. From the fifth century BC different philosophical schools arose in China focusing on the meaning and role of the Dao, and by the second century AD Daoism had emerged as a distinct religion.

*The Dao*
It is said the Dao existed from the beginning of time without form or shape. The Dao gave birth to "the One", the origin, and this divided to produce the material forces. Everything that was clear and luminous drifted to the heavens, and everything that was dark and heavy sank to the earth. The essences of heaven and earth are *yin* and *yang* – the natural forces that interact dynamically to create all life. *Yin* is cool, fluid, and feminine, while *yang* is hot, dry, and masculine; the two forces continually rise and fall in relation to each other. The *yin/yang* balance can be disrupted by human behaviour, but ritual and prayer can help to restore it.

### *Qi*: the life force

Daoists believe that *qi* (*ch'i*) is the energy that shapes all forms and animates all life. To maintain maximum health in the land and rivers, or in the human body, *qi* needs to flow smoothly. When it is blocked, illness or stagnation can result. Chinese medicine focuses on the even flow of *qi* and the correct balance of *yin* and *yang* in the body. *Feng shui* focuses on the beneficial flow of *qi* and the *yin/yang* interaction in the landscape – it identifies where *qi* may be dispersing too quickly, or accumulating and decaying.

## Deities and immortals

Beliefs in the supernatural world, originating in shamanism, continue to exist in Daoism, and deities or immortal beings are called upon to help in times of need. The Daoist pantheon has hundreds of deities protecting all aspects of life, from the Jade Emperor, ruler of heaven, to gods of kitchens, doors, and walls, or gods of health, wealth, and prosperity.

The Eight Immortals of Daoism, who reflect the Daoist quest to achieve physical immortality, are particularly popular. Known for their magical powers, humour, unpredictability, and wisdom, they rescue those in need and punish the wicked. Their stories are often repeated when families honour their ancestors at the Qingming festival.

# Hinduism

Hindus call their religion *Sanatana Dharma* or "eternal truth". It has developed in India over millennia and is rich in beliefs, rituals, and traditions. Although there are a multitude of gods and goddesses, Hindus believe they are all aspects of Brahman, the Supreme Being. It is the yearning of the individual's soul – a divine spark – to become one with Brahman, the universal soul. The Hindu journey is the journey of the soul through countless deaths and rebirths until it finds liberation from the endless cycle of rebirth and sinks back into Brahman.

*Dharma* encompasses several meanings. It is the eternal truth or law, it is the correct order that sustains the universe, and it is the duty of each Hindu to fulfil their religious, social, and ethical obligations – to follow their *dharma*.

## Beginnings

"Hindu" was the name historically given by outsiders to the people living around the Sindhu (Indus) River, which has its source in Tibet and flows out through Pakistan. There is archaeological evidence of a flourishing and stable civilization in the Indus valley from the third millennium BC. This civilization then went into decline and was overtaken by Aryans, a branch of the Indo-European peoples of central Asia. The Aryans, a semi-nomadic warrior tribe, migrated down from Iran to settle and eventually merge with the people and culture of the Indus valley.

There are around 950 million Hindus worldwide and almost all live in south Asia. The population of India is over 80 per cent Hindu.

## Hindu beliefs

Hindus believe that the universe is continually being created, sustained, and eventually destroyed for a new one to arise. The universe passes through lesser cycles within greater cycles for all eternity. Hindus say we are currently in a lesser cycle called Kali Yuga, a time of darkness. This is an age of injustice, conflict, and decay that has lasted for thousands of years, but in time it will end, ushering in an age of peace, justice, and wisdom.

### Atman: the individual soul

The cycles of life, death, and rebirth are not only reflected in the enormity of the universe but also within day-to-day life. Everything is subject to change, but the *atman*, the divine spark, is unchanging. Until an individual gains the wisdom to understand they are identical with Brahman, they will keep on being reborn in different forms, forever tied into *samsara*, the wheel of rebirth. Through positive actions, devotion, and true knowledge of Brahman, the individual soul will find release and rebirth will cease.

The inseparable relationship between the individual soul – *atman* – and the universal soul – Brahman – is expressed in the phrase *tat tvam asi* or "you (*atman*) are that (Brahman)".

## Karma: cause and effect

*Karma* is the law of cause and effect, the idea that every action bears "fruit" in this life or the next. Positive and unselfish actions accumulate good *karma*, while hurtful or destructive actions accumulate negative *karma*. People who are just and truthful, who fulfil their religious duties, will experience a better rebirth. Those who cause suffering, who act selfishly or immorally, may be born into a life of poverty, pain, or neglect in human or other forms.

## Moksha: liberation

*Moksha* is release; it is liberation from the wheel of *samsara*. If the journey of the soul is hampered by *karma* it will keep passing from one life to the next, but when the soul has broken the karmic ties, it achieves *moksha* – union with Brahman.

The principles of *karma*, reincarnation, and liberation from the cycles of birth and death are also found in Buddhism and Jainism, which originated in India. However, the way in which these principles are understood or realized is different in each religious tradition. Belief in the *atman* finding union with Brahman is only found within Hinduism.

## Hindu gods

Hindus believe that Brahman is the indestructible energy that sustains the universe. The Upanishads, part of the ancient scriptures, say that words cannot be found to describe the full nature of Brahman – an awestruck "Ah" is the most accurate expression. Brahman is the essence of the universe, the power that enables the mind to feel and understand. Brahman is God, the universal soul or ultimate reality that has always existed and will always exist.

Hindus believe that all things are expressions of Brahman – from gods and goddesses to humans, from tiny creatures to the earth itself. In the eternal spiritual realm that is free from suffering, there is no male or female as everything is in full union with Brahman.

There are many Hindu deities. Some are linked to particular communities or places and worshipped locally; others are the focus of devotion for Hindus in India and beyond.

### Brahma, Vishnu, and Shiva

Brahman creates, sustains, and destroys the material world by assuming different forms. The triumvirate of Brahma, Vishnu, and Shiva symbolize this eternal cycle of change. Through the form of Brahma the world comes into being; through the form of Vishnu it is sustained; and through the form of Shiva the world is destroyed in order for creation to begin again in a never-ending cycle. Sometimes Brahma, Vishnu, and Shiva are represented in paintings and statues as three faces on one body – this is called the *Trimurti* or "three forms".

**Avatars**

*Avatar* means "one who descends". Hindus believe that God appears on earth as an avatar when goodness and truth need to be upheld and evil conquered. Vishnu has ten avatars, the most popular ones being Rama and Krishna. Vishnu's final avatar, Kalki, has yet to come, and Hindus believe he will appear in triumph at the end of this age to usher in a time of justice and purity.

## Lakshmi, Ganesh, and Hanuman

Lakshmi, the beautiful wife of Vishnu and goddess of fortune, is believed to bestow prosperity on those who pray to her. She is a soothing and protective deity who embodies the love that comes from total devotion to God. She is a favourite household goddess in many Hindu homes and is particularly popular among women. Lakshmi reflects the feminine aspect of God – the spiritual energy that purifies the individual.

The much-loved elephant-headed god Ganesh is believed to be the remover of obstacles, protecting those who start fresh ventures, begin journeys, or ask for blessings at the beginning of each new day. His picture is often found in homes, businesses, and offices. This son of Shiva and Parvati is also worshipped as the bringer of knowledge and has a special place in the devotions of students. Ganesh is often depicted with a small mouse near his feet representing selfishness or desires that must be overcome to gain wisdom.

Hanuman, the popular monkey-headed god, is renowned for his physical and mental strength, perseverance, and unrelenting devotion. He represents loyalty to the service of God. In the epic *Ramayana* he searches for Rama's abducted wife, courageously facing all challenges obstructing his way. Later in the story Hanuman lifts a Himalayan mountain on his shoulders and flies to Rama's wounded brother so the healing herbs growing on its slopes can cure his battle wounds.

## Hindu scriptures

Hindu scriptures encompass hymns and poems, chants, and ritual guides, from complex philosophical texts to great epic stories. They are written in Sanskrit, the sacred language of ancient India.

Hindu scriptures are divided into two groups – *shruti* (heard) and *smriti* (remembered). Scriptures believed to be revealed by God to sages are *shruti*; those handed down orally over the centuries before being written down are *smriti*. The Vedas are considered *shruti* and the later epics and Puranas are *smriti*.

## The Vedas

The oldest Hindu texts are called the Vedas – *veda* means "knowledge". First written down towards the end of the second millennium BC, they belong to a much older oral tradition. There are four Vedas: Rig-Veda, Sama-Veda, Yajur-Veda, and Atharva-Veda. The best-known text is the Rig-Veda, containing hymns to the earliest Hindu gods.

## The Upanishads

The Upanishads appear at the end of each Veda and belong to a later period of history. The secret meaning within them was given by teachers to their students – the word *upanishad* means "sitting near" – and the text is written as dialogues. These scriptures contain ideas on reincarnation, the soul's liberation from the cycles of birth, death, and rebirth, and the relationship between the soul and Brahman.

## The Puranas

Meaning "ancient history", the Puranas record the stories of the gods based around Brahma, Vishnu, and Shiva. The combination of myths, legends, and historical material made the Puranas more accessible to ordinary Hindus who were not familiar with the more scholarly scriptures contained in the Vedas.

## Epic poems

The *Mahabarata*, the epic of the "Bharatas", tells the story of two powerful warring families. It was written

from the end of the first millennium BC. Within it is
the Bhagavad-Gita, or "Song of the Lord", one of the
most influential Hindu texts dealing with the meaning
and purpose of life. It is the conversation between
the hero of the story, Arjuna, and his charioteer, the
god Krishna. Even though Arjuna is unwilling to kill
in battle, Krishna tells him it is his duty, his *dharma*.
Whatever may happen, the souls of those who die
are indestructible. The Bhagavad-Gita then explains
the intense love of God for humanity – a love that can
be personally and powerfully experienced through
devotion or *bhakti*.

The *Ramayana* is a much-loved epic poem
encompassing the ideals of a Hindu life – duty,
morality, love, loyalty, and courage. It tells the story
of Rama's struggle to find and release his wife, Sita,
who has been captured by the demon, Ravana. It
represents the triumph of truth and justice over evil,
and the events of the *Ramayana* are frequently told and
re-enacted.

## Hindu practice
*Aum*, also spelled *Om*, is believed to be the sound of
God – the source of all sound. It is the sound within
time and beyond time. *Om* is said at the beginning and
end of worship, and is used in hymns and chants.

### Worship in the home
The deity or deities in a Hindu home are treated with
great respect, and daily worship, or *puja*, is offered

to them. The shrine could be on a shelf, in a quiet corner, or could occupy a whole room, but what is important is the devotion and love that is expressed during *puja*. Each day the deities are ritually bathed and offered food, incense, and flowers. They are often gently touched with sandalwood paste and coloured powders. Accompanied by prayers or chants, a ghee lamp is moved in a clockwise motion in front of the deities – this is the *arti* ceremony. The lamp is also moved among the worshippers, who hold their hands over its flame then touch their foreheads and eyes to receive God's blessing.

Cleanliness and ritual purification play an important role in Hindu practice. Hindus bathe before worship and water is used to wash shrine and temple deities. Bottles of water from the sacred River Ganges are often placed before shrines, and Hindus ritually bathe in sacred rivers.

## Worship in the temple

There are thousands of temples of all sizes throughout towns and villages in India, some attracting thousands of visitors each day and hundreds of thousands at festival time, while others might be local to a village. At the heart of the temple is the inner shrine where the main temple deity is housed and tended by a temple priest, or *pujari*, who leads the worship. Temple deities are carefully bathed, dressed, and prepared before the shrine curtains are opened to reveal them to the gathered worshippers. Being in the presence of the deities in this way is called *darshan* – a direct and intimate way of seeing and being seen by God.

## Paths to God

Hindus believe there are different paths to God and it is up to the individual to choose the one that is right for them. Each path is a way to journey closer to Brahman and understand the nature of God.

- *Bhakti* is the path of devotion – a way to experience God's profound love through total faith and trust. Devotees have a direct and joyful relationship with God through a personal deity such as Krishna or Rama.

- *Karma* is the path of action, of performing positive, just, and selfless actions in society. These works create positive *karma* for the individual and for society.

- *Jnana* is the path of knowledge – the study of scriptures to understand the truth behind them, to come closer to experiencing God. A guru is needed to guide Hindus along this path.

- *Yoga* unites physical and spiritual forces to discipline the mind. Yoga techniques include Hathayoga, Dhyanayoga, and Rajayoga.

## Rites of passage

A Hindu life is marked by rites called *samskaras*.
They begin before birth and end at death; they not
only mark stages within an individual's life but also
strengthen family and community bonds. There are
traditionally sixteen *samskaras*, but many Hindus do
not experience them all.

Most families will carry out a set of rituals around
the birth of a child and its early months of life. Around
the age of twelve boys from the Brahmin, Kshatriya,
and Vaishya social classes will undergo the sacred
thread ceremony to mark their passage into the adult
world and the religious and social responsibilities this
entails. There are also marriage rites and, finally, rites
surrounding death.

### *Birth*

In preparation for the birth, the mother may read
Hindu scriptures to the unborn child for health and
blessings. A naming ceremony is held ten or twelve
days after birth, and the parents may take the baby
briefly out of the home for the first time, although the
scriptures recommend the fourth month. At around
six months the baby has their first taste of solid food
during morning worship. At the age of one, or in
their third or fifth year, boys have their first haircut
to remove symbolically negative *karma* carried over
from a previous life. In some parts of India, girls also
undergo this *samskara*.

## *Marriage*

Parents traditionally find a partner for their child with the consent of the son or daughter through a network of contacts. The preparations and traditions surrounding the union may vary within communities, but the marriage itself takes place around a sacred fire and is officiated by a Hindu priest. The marriage is not binding until seven steps have been completed around the sacred fire, the couple reciting a vow at each step.

## *Death*

In the last stage of life prayers are said or hymns chanted to ease the dying, and drops of water from the sacred River Ganges may be trickled into the mouth. At death, the body is bathed, wrapped in a new cloth, and taken in procession to a funeral pyre or to a crematorium. The indestructible soul will continue its journey to the next rebirth. The family collects the ashes and bones after cremation and will try to scatter them on the sea or a river, particularly the River Ganges.

## **Structure of society and phases of life**

The term "Varnashrama-dharma" encompasses the social order and responsibilities of Hindu life. The *varnas* are the social classes, the *ashramas* are the stages of life, and the *dharma* is religious and social duty, and unchanging law.

*Varnas*

Early Vedic scriptures divided Hindu society into four
social classes that worked in harmony with each other
to uphold order and truth within society. The Brahmins
were the priests, the Kshatriyas were the warriors and
rulers, the Vaishyas were the merchants, and the Shudras
were the craftspeople and manual workers. There
remained a class of people outside these four groups
who carried out society's most menial work. They
formed the "untouchable" castes and call themselves
*Dalit*, or "downtrodden". This group, who constitute
more than 16 per cent of the Indian population, are the
most underprivileged section of society.

With each social class or *varna* there are hundreds
of castes that are further divided into many sub-castes.
They are determined by birth, can be created through
intermarriage, and are often linked to occupation.
They create supportive social and economic networks
but can also be a source of tension or conflict.

*Ashramas*

The life of a male is traditionally divided into four
stages called *ashramas*, although some do not enter all
stages. Women are traditionally regarded as dependent
upon male family members, but they play a pivotal role
in the social and religious life of the family.

> **Brahmacharya-ashrama** (the student): a boy enters
> the first stage of study and learns the duties of
> adult Hindu life.

*Grihastha-ashrama* (the householder): a man marries and sets up home, taking responsibility for providing for his family, educating children, and carrying out religious duties in the home and community.

*Vanaprastha-ashrama* (the forest dweller): a man withdraws from family duties and hands them over to the next generation. Some may leave home, but many remain and dedicate time to the study of scriptures, charitable causes, and community work.

*Sanyasa-ashrama* (the holy man): all worldly ties are renounced so the man becomes a wandering ascetic whose main goal is to achieve *moksha*, union with God.

## Hindu festivals

The Hindu year is rich in colourful festivals associated with deities, stories, events, and seasons. Some are widely celebrated by Hindus, although the rituals may vary, while others might be particular to a community or region. The Hindu calendar follows the lunar year, with an intercalary month added every two to three years to keep in step with the solar calendar.

## Widely celebrated festivals

**Sarasvati Puja:** the goddess of learning and the arts is honoured and the beginning of spring is celebrated in northern India.

**Mahashivaratri**: the Great Night of Shiva is observed with twenty-four hours of fasting and special *puja* to Shiva.

**Holi**: the festival honours Vishnu's protective powers and also celebrates the grain harvest with bonfires and the boisterous throwing of coloured water and powder.

**Rama Naumi**: Rama's birthday is recalled with a reading of the *Ramayana*, and a model of the baby Rama in a cradle is set up in the temple.

**Raksha Bandhan**: bonds of love and protection are strengthened as sisters tie *rakhis*, coloured threads, around their brothers' wrists.

**Janmashtami**: at midnight, after a day of fasting and prayer, an image of Krishna as a baby is rocked in a cradle to commemorate his birth.

**Durga Puja or Navaratri**: Devi, the mother goddess and female aspect of divine power, is celebrated in her different forms over nine nights.

**Dussehra**: this festival falls the day immediately after Navaratri. It honours Devi in the form of Durga. The celebrations recall her triumph over the demon Mahishasura and Rama's slaying of the demon Ravana.

**Divali**: the festival of lights begins at the end of the month of Aswin and lasts up to five days. Divali derives from *Deepavali*, meaning row of lights. *Divas*, small clay lamps lit with ghee, are lined along windows, walls, and courtyards, and strings of brightly coloured lights decorate homes while fireworks light up the night. This festival welcomes the goddess Lakshmi, bringer of prosperity, into homes and businesses. It also celebrates the conquest of good over evil represented by the triumphant return of Rama and Sita after Rama defeated the demon Ravana. For many Hindus, Divali traditionally marks the end of the financial year, and a fresh start is made on a financial and personal level.

## Hindu pilgrimage

Millions of Hindus go on pilgrimage throughout the year for different reasons – to thank God for blessings, to pray for a special request, to celebrate a festival, to visit a famous temple, or to pray at a site associated with a favourite deity. Pilgrimage accumulates merit and is an important part of Hindu devotion – it brings the pilgrim closer to the divine.

Among the thousands of Hindu pilgrimage sites are temples, sacred rivers, and mountains. Krishna is linked to the town of Vrindavan on the banks of the River Yamuna – Krishna spent his childhood in an ancient forest here and it is said he never leaves Vrindavan. Shiva is believed to sit in meditation on the Himalayan summit of Mount Kailas and uses his long matted hair to control the mighty flow of the Ganges as it tumbles out of the mountain range.

The seven sacred rivers of India are the Ganges, Yamuna, Narmada, Godavari, Kaveri, Sindhu, and the legendary Sarasvati. Each one is associated with a deity.

### The sacred River Ganges

Flowing from its source in the remote Himalayas to the Bay of Bengal, the Ganges is India's most sacred river, honoured as the goddess Ganga on earth. The god Shiva is believed to have lived in Varanasi, the ancient holy city on its banks in Uttar Pradesh state. Millions of Hindus come here to bathe and offer *puja*, symbolically cleansing themselves in its sacred waters.

The dead are burnt on cremation *ghats*, stone platforms at the river's edge – it is the wish of Hindus to die here and have their ashes scattered on the waters.

# Islam

The word "Islam" means peace and submission; Muslims greet one another in the name of peace, *Assalamu Alaikum*, which means, "peace with you". Islam is a way of life built on a belief in one God who revealed his word through the prophet Muhammad. Muslims speak of five practices called Five Pillars that uphold their faith.

## Beginnings

According to tradition, Muhammad was born in AD 570 in Mecca at a time when the Saudi region was populated by many tribes, most of them polytheistic. Orphaned at a young age, he was entrusted to the care of his uncle, a trader. At twenty-five he married a wealthy widow, Kadijah, who had employed him as her representative in trade. People often consulted him to settle disputes because of his reputation for integrity.

Muhammad became increasingly unhappy with the idolatry and moral corruption of Meccan society and often retreated to the mountains. It was there in the cave at Hira in AD 610 that he received the first of many revelations calling him to worship one God, Allah. At first he told only Kadijah and close friends, but then he began preaching against the evils of society and created enemies among the merchants.

The year AD 622 marked a turning point.
Muhammad and his followers fled from persecution
to seek refuge in the city of Medina where there were
already some Muslims and hospitable Jews. It was in
Medina that Muhammad built the first mosque and
where he created an army, believing that fighting
in self-defence was the will of Allah. A period of
warfare followed until the Muslims marched into
and peaceably occupied Mecca on 1 January 630.
Muhammad died in 631.

In Islam only Allah is worshipped. Muhammad is
believed to be a man who lived and died. Muslims say,
"Peace be upon him" as an honorific when they say
his name.

Allah was already worshipped as the creator
God when Muhammad began preaching, but he was
worshipped as one god among many. Muhammad's
radical message was that Allah was the one and only
God. He believed Allah to be the same God who was
worshipped by Christians and Jews, calling them the
people of the book, and claiming continuity with them.

## Sources

Sources for the life of Muhammad are the Quran
itself and the *hadith* – traditional accounts and
sayings that were learnt verbatim and transmitted
orally at a time when accurate memory was
highly prized. Each *hadith* has a record of those

who passed the saying along. One of the first collections was that of the ninth-century Persian scholar al-Bukhari who rejected those *hadith* that did not have a reliable chain of transmission.

## The spread of Islam

The period after Muhammad's death was one of quarrels within the community and fighting without as Islam became established under the Umayyad dynasty in Syria and then the Abbasid dynasty in Baghdad. It was taken via conquest and trade as far afield as China and Indonesia as well as across to Spain and into Africa.

There are over 1.3 billion Muslims in the world today with Indonesia having the largest Muslim population.

## The Sunni/Shia divide

The major division in Islam is between Sunni and Shia although both follow the Five Pillars. The division originated in a dispute about whether Muhammad's successor, the first caliph, should be his companion, Abu Bakr, or his cousin and son-in-law, Ali. The question hinged on whether the successor should be chosen by the community as a civil as well as spiritual leader (Sunni) or should be a spiritual leader from the family of the prophet (Shia). Around 85 per cent of Muslims are Sunni and 15 per cent Shia. There are further divisions within Shia, each group having its

own spiritual leader. Shia often pray at the shrines of
Muslim saints.

Sufism is a mystical path in Islam with both Sunni
and Shia adherents. Sufis follow spiritual practices to
surrender the self to Allah.

---

### The Muslim calendar

The Muslim calendar dates from the year of
the *Hijra*, the migration of Muhammad and
his followers to Medina in AD 622. It is a lunar
calendar based on twelve cycles of the moon, so
each year is about ten days shorter than a solar
calendar. This is why festivals and the month of
fasting occur earlier each year according to the
Western calendar.

---

## The first pillar: the *shahadah*

*La ilaha illa Allah wa-Muhammad rasul Allah.*
*"There is no god but God, and Muhammad is his*
*messenger."*

Belief in and declaration of the *shahadah* is what
makes a Muslim. Muslims believe there is only one
omnipotent, transcendent creator God and nothing
and no one else must be worshipped. The habitual
saying, *Inshallah* – "if Allah wills" – when speaking

about the future acknowledges that Allah is in control of all things. *Allah* is the Arabic word for "one God, creator of the universe". As Arabic is regarded as the language of heaven, Muslims usually call God "Allah" even when speaking another language.

Worship of any object or any being is *shirk* and absolutely forbidden. Disobeying the Quran, the holy scriptures believed to be the word of God, is a form of *shirk* as is valuing a person or object above Allah. Images of Allah are strictly forbidden, as are images of living beings. Instead mosques and many homes are adorned with geometric or floral patterns or pictures of the Kaaba, the sacred stone in Mecca.

### Ninety-nine names for Allah

The Quran contains ninety-name names for Allah, which reveal his character. These include:

- Al-Khaliq – the Creator
- Al-Alim – the All Knowing
- Al-Hafiz – the Preserver
- Al-Haqq – the Truth
- Al-Mani – the Preventer of Harm.

Muslims often use a string of ninety-nine or thirty-three beads to meditate on the names of Allah.

> Some Muslim boys' names include the attributes of Allah, such as the following:
>
> - Abdul Kabir – servant of the Most Great
> - Abdul-Rahmin – servant of the Most Compassionate One
> - Abdul-Malik – servant of the Lord.

## Angels and jinn

According to Islam, Allah created an unseen world of angels and jinn. Angels, made from light, always obey Allah and do his will on earth. They keep a record of the good and bad deeds of each person in preparation for the Day of Judgment. *Jinns* have free will, are made from smokeless fire, and often defy Allah, causing mischief. Iblis, the devil, is said to be a *jinn* who would not prostrate himself before Allah.

## Holy scriptures

Muslims believe the Quran is the direct eternal word of Allah revealed to Muhammad in a series of revelations that were collected together to form the Quran.

It is divided into 116 *surahs*, or chapters, each one believed to be a separate revelation. With the exception of the first *surah*, they are arranged according to length – the second *surah* is the longest; the final *surah* is the shortest. This aids learning the Quran by heart, a skill highly valued in Islam. Children often go daily to mosque schools (*madrassahs*) to learn to read the Quran in Arabic.

Many of the key people of Judaism and Christianity appear in the Quran and are believed to be prophets of Islam. They include Adam, Nuh (Noah), Ibrahim (Abraham), Ishmael, Ishaq (Isaac), Yousef (Joseph), Yunus (Jonah), Yahya (John), and Isa (Jesus).

The Quran teaches that Jesus was born of a virgin but categorically denies that he was the Son of God. It also denies that Jesus was crucified, though it acknowledges people plotted against him.

The Quran is believed to be the final revelation of Allah, correcting misconceptions that are believed to have arisen about earlier prophets such as Jesus. Muhammad is thus known as the "Seal of the Prophets".

Copies of the Quran are treated with great respect. Book rests are used for study and Qurans are never placed on the floor. Muslims wash ritually before touching its pages. When not in use the Quran is wrapped in clean cloths or an embroidered cover and put on a high shelf: the words of the Quran should always be above all other words in the room.

## Muslim ethics

All Muslim ethics are derived ultimately from the Quran. It is called the "Book of Guidance" because it is believed to contain a divinely ordered pattern for the individual and society, called the *Sharia*. Individuals are not allowed to interpret the Quran for themselves but are expected to act according to principles of interpretation laid down by *Sharia* scholars. *Sharia* law covers all aspects of life. There are four basic sources for *Sharia*:

- The Quran.
- The *Sunna* of the prophet Muhammad (*Sunna* means "trodden path"). Muslims believe that Muhammad lived in full submission to Allah and showed perfectly how to interpret the Quran.
- The consensus of the Muslim community.
- Reasoning based on principles of analogy.

There are four different schools of law for interpreting *Sharia* within Sunni Islam. Shia look to their spiritual leaders and the Jafari school of law for guidance and interpretation.

Forgiveness is an important part of Muslim ethics. Allah forgives those who truly repent, and Muslims are exhorted not to take revenge on those who have offended them but to forgive instead.

The struggle between the desire to do good and the desire to do evil is called *jihad*. *Jihad* also refers to holy war, but Muhammad believed that this inner struggle was the greater one.

### *Haram* and *halal*
All actions are divided into *haram* (forbidden) and *halal* (permitted).

Actions that are *haram* include:

• Murder, theft, and lying
• Eating pork or other products made from pig meat or an animal not ritually slaughtered
• Drinking alcohol
• Lending money to gain interest.

*Halal* covers actions that are prescribed, such as kindness to neighbours, following the Five Pillars, and those actions that are not explicitly prohibited, such as driving cars.

## The second pillar: *salat*

*Salat* is the recitation of set prayers five times daily, beginning before sunrise and ending after dusk. The other prayer times are spaced between the two and may be grouped together.

Muslims say that the command to pray five times a day was given by Allah to Muhammad in a night vision in which he flew on a winged horse to Jerusalem and ascended through the seven heavens to Paradise.

Traditionally a *muezzin* has the job of calling Muslims to prayer. He stands at the top of a minaret, a tall tower attached to the mosque, and his voice rings out across the village or city, perhaps aided nowadays by loudspeakers. In the modern world many Muslims have alarm computer software that alerts them to prayer times, or that recites the call to prayer at the correct time. The call to prayer, or *adhan*, begins, *Allahu Akbar*: "God is great."

Prayers are said facing the direction of the Kaaba in Mecca, with prayer mats often used to make a clean place for prayer. Prayer involves bowing, prostration, sitting back on one's heels, and standing. Ritual washing (*wudu*) precedes prayer, and shoes are removed and heads are covered. At the end of each prayer time there is a time for personal prayers. Muslims often pray at other times to express concerns, make requests, and give thanks.

The main prayer time of the week is Friday lunchtime. These prayers are known as the *Juma* prayers. Men sometimes go to the mosque to pray during the week. At Friday prayers the *imam*, the mosque leader, gives a sermon often linking the Quran with contemporary events. Friday prayers end with the shaking of hands to mark the shared sense of community.

### The Kaaba

Within the huge courtyard of the Grand Mosque, Masjid al-Haram, in Mecca is the Kaaba, a black cuboid building with a single room inside, its doorway draped with an embroidered cloth.

Embedded in the south-east corner is a black meteorite said to have been kissed by Muhammad and, some say, brought by Adam from Paradise. Neither the stone nor the Kaaba are worshipped – they serve to unite Muslims in prayer. There is a tradition that says that whatever is wished for on first sight of the Kaaba will be granted.

## Inside the mosque

The qibla is the direction that Muslims face when praying towards the Kaaba. Mosques have a qibla wall, which often has a concave section to indicate the direction of prayer. The *minbar* is a stepped pulpit from which the *imam* delivers his sermon. A clock with six faces shows prayer times for the day and the time of the *Juma* prayers for that week.

Carpets in the main prayer hall often have straight lines to facilitate standing in rows shoulder to shoulder. Men and women pray separately and are generally divided so they cannot see one another. The women's prayer section of the mosque is usually smaller because they often stay at home with the children, who are primarily their responsibility.

The mosque is often a centre for the Muslim community and an organization for pastoral care. Some mosques also have morgues where bodies are prepared for burial.

Washing in preparation for prayer (*wudu*) must

be completed in a set order and begins with saying
*Bismillah* – "In the name of Allah". It covers those parts
of the body exposed to dirt and grime: hands, mouth,
nostrils, face, arms, head, ears, and feet. An ablution
can last a number of prayers but is made invalid by
certain actions, including falling asleep and urinating.

In cool countries mosques usually have places
for *wudu* inside. In hotter countries these are often
outside.

## The third pillar: *zakat*

*Zakat* refers to the obligation that Muslims have to help
the poor through charitable giving. Muslims give 2.5
per cent of the worth of their assets to the poor every
year. This includes the worth of property as well as
money in the bank. The annual tax is paid during the
festival of Eid ul-Fitr. Money or food is also given to
the poor to mark other times, such as the birth of a
child or when going on pilgrimage. It is believed that
ultimately everything belongs to Allah. People act as
his vice-regents and should use their assets wisely
and according to principles laid down in the Quran.

## The fourth pillar: *sawm*

*Sawm* refers to the practice of fasting. Muslims fast
during the month of Ramadan. No food or liquid may
pass the lips from before sunrise until sunset. Sexual
intercourse is also prohibited during daylight hours.
Eating and drinking are permitted if a person is
pregnant, ill, or travelling. Missed days are made up at

another time or money is given to the poor. Two main reasons given for the purpose of fasting are learning self-discipline and identifying with the poor. Dates are usually eaten at the breaking of the fast, which is called Iftar.

The month is a holy one with an emphasis on prayer and reading of the Quran. Traditionally the twenty-seventh night of Ramadan is the Night of Power, a remembrance of the first revelation to Muhammad. Many stay up all night reading the Quran and praying together in community.

Eid ul-Fitr or the lesser Eid celebrates the end of Ramadan, and families and friends get together. There are new clothes, children are often given presents, and *zakat* is paid.

## The fifth pillar: *Hajj*
The final pillar is the *Hajj*, pilgrimage to Mecca at least once in a lifetime by all Muslims who can afford it, who have fulfilled family duties, and who are fit enough to undertake it. The pilgrimage is a communal event, taking place in the month of Dhu al-Hijjah, the twelfth and final month of the Muslim year when nearly 3 million Muslims pour into Mecca. It is a time of equality, prayer, and repentance.

As the *Hajj* draws to a close Muslims all over the world celebrate the greater Eid: Eid ul-Adha. An animal, usually a goat or sheep, is sacrificed and shared with the poor. Nowadays butchers often perform the task and money may be given instead of actual meat.

Only Muslims may go on *Hajj* or visit the Grand Mosque that contains the Kaaba. There are signs in Mecca directing Muslims towards the Kaaba and non-Muslims away from it.

The *Hajj* recalls some of the story of the prophet Ibrahim (Abraham). One of the rituals associated with the *Hajj* involves pilgrims running back and forth between two hills. This act is a reminder of when Ibrahim's second wife, Hajar, was alone in the desert, running around desperately seeking water for her baby son, Ishmael. When Ishmael ground his foot into the sand a spring of water appeared. This is known as the Zamzam Well, and pilgrims continue to visit the well to drink its water. The sacrifice of an animal recalls Ibrahim's obedience to Allah in being prepared to sacrifice his son, Ishmael. Instead Allah provided a ram.

## The cycle of life

The cycle of a Muslim's life reflects the submission to Allah and his will in the Quran.

### Birth

According to Islam all babies are born obeying Allah. The father whispers the words of the *Adhan*, the call to prayer, in the baby's ear. The baby's parents give money to the poor. Boys are circumcised – the timing of circumcision depends on the tradition. It is common to shave the baby's head and give the weight in silver as charity.

Muslims call people who become Muslims "reverts", because it is believed they are returning to where they began at birth – obeying Allah.

## Marriage

Marriage is a contract of mutual commitment between a man and woman before at least two witnesses and is believed to be pleasing to Allah. It is normally arranged by the parents but, according to the Quran, must be undertaken with the woman's consent. The groom gives the bride a *mahr*, a sum of money or goods, which are hers alone and remain hers if there is a divorce. Ceremonies often include separate parties for the sexes but vary according to the country and tradition. Men may take up to four wives if they can provide for them. In general, divorce is permitted but frowned upon. Women must wait three months after divorce before remarrying to identify who is the father of any child she is carrying.

Men and women are believed to be equal but different. Women are responsible for the home, though many also work outside the home. Men are expected to provide for their wives and children, including following a divorce.

### Hijab

*Hijab* is the principle of dressing modestly for both men and women but has also come to mean women covering their head in the company of men who are not closely related. The *hijab* has also become a sign of commitment and identity. Some Muslim women wear a *niqab*, a veil that covers the face, as part of *hijab*.

## Death

The timing and manner of death is believed to be the will of Allah and is not viewed as accidental. It is said that the Angel of Death comes for the individual when Allah wills. Muslims are encouraged to think of Allah at the point of death, which is not the end; this mortal life is seen as preparation for the next immortal one and death is but sleeping until the Day of Judgment. The body is washed, scented, and prepared for burial by family of the same gender or people appointed by the mosque. It is not left alone and is treated with great dignity. During the preparation ritual prayers are said. Muslims are never cremated, but buried in a white sheet or sheets and without any possessions, as soon as possible after the death. The body is laid on its right side to face Mecca. Muslims believe that on the Day of Judgment all will be raised – the unrighteous will go to hell, and the righteous will go to Paradise to be with Allah.

# Jainism

*Jain* means "follower of the Jina" or "one who overcomes" – the title given to someone who has attained infinite and perfect knowledge. Jainism is one of the ancient religions of India.

Jains believe that the universe follows its own cosmic laws and cannot be created or destroyed. All substances in the universe may modify or change their form, just as the human form changes from childhood to old age, but the soul, or *jiva*, is permanent and imperishable. Souls are trapped in the cycles of birth, death, and rebirth because of attachment to the material world – they have limited vision and knowledge.

The soul accumulates a spiritual residue, or *karma*, through negative actions, greed, and ignorance. This karmic matter binds the soul to rebirth, but non-violence, good conduct, and wisdom free it from *karma*. With release from *karma*, the soul achieves *kevala* – it has perfect vision and knowledge. At death the soul will be finally liberated to live in a state of bliss called *siddha*.

## Non-violence

Jains follow the principle of *ahimsa*, or non-violence,
in body and mind. They avoid killing or injuring living
creatures, and they try to abstain from behaviour and
occupations that are damaging or hurtful to others and
oneself. Jain monks and nuns are particularly strict
and carry a small brush to sweep the path ahead in
case they stand on insects. Some wear a small mask
over their mouth and nose to protect insects that might
otherwise fly in.

There are 4.6 million Jains worldwide. The majority,
over 4.4 million, live in India, but there are also
sizeable communities in the USA, Kenya, the UK,
Tanzania, and Nepal.

## Beginnings

Jains believe the universe passes through cycles, and
a succession of twenty-four great teachers called
*Tirthankaras* appear in each cycle. *Tirthankara* means
"bridge-maker" since these great teachers set an
example of non-violence and generosity, helping
people cross from ignorance to knowledge.

The final *Tirthankara* to appear in the current cycle
was born in 599 BC near Patna in north-east India, and
given the title *Mahavira* or "Great Victor". At the age
of thirty he became a wandering ascetic, renouncing
physical comforts and focusing on his spiritual
journey. After twelve years he realized *kevala* – infinite
knowledge and complete detachment from worldly

desires. He began teaching others and led the Jain community of monks, nuns, and lay people.

After Mahavira's death Jains divided into two groups: Shvetambaras or "white clad", after the colour of robes worn by monks and nuns, and Digambaras or "sky clad", because male ascetics are naked (although robes are now sometimes worn in public).

## Jain *puja*

Eight different materials are used during *puja* (worship) at a shrine or at home. During the ritual Jains reflect on the symbolism of each substance:

- **Water**: the journey across the ocean of life, death, and rebirth to achieve liberation
- **Sandalwood**: the path of knowledge
- **Flower**: good conduct and compassion to all living beings
- **Incense**: striving towards an ascetic life
- **Candle**: the soul that has been liberated from *karma*
- **Rice**: making this life the last birth before finding liberation
- **Sweet food**: weakening attachment to the pleasures of life
- **Fruit**: the fruit of *moksha*, final release from *karma*.

## The Five Vows

The ethical code of Jainism is summed up in the Five Vows that are followed by the monastic community and lay people:

- Non-violence (*ahimsa*)
- Truthfulness
- Non-stealing
- Non-possession
- Chastity (meaning fidelity for married couples and celibacy for monks and nuns)

# Judaism

Judaism is an inheritance: a Jew is someone born of a Jewish mother. For religious Jews – sometimes known as observant Jews – it is a way of life in obedience to the one God. Some people choose to follow the way of life by conversion.

## Beginnings

The historic roots of Judaism lie in the Near East. The Torah, the sacred text, tells how Jews became a people chosen by God to serve him. The patriarch Abraham was called by God to leave his home in the city of Ur with his family and livestock to worship God. There in the desert God made a covenant with Abraham – he would be his God and Abraham and all his descendants would be God's people, and God promised Abraham a land.

Exodus, the second book of the Torah, gives an account of Moses, who was called by God to lead Abraham's descendants out of Egypt. They had moved there in a time of famine and had become enslaved. The people eventually settled in the land of Canaan, which they claimed as the Promised Land. This area is now known as Palestine or Israel. It was frequently occupied by foreign powers and the leaders were sent into exile.

**The Western Wall**

One wall remains of the Temple rebuilt by King Herod on the site believed by Jews to be the original site of a great temple built by Solomon in the tenth century BC. It was destroyed by the Romans in AD 70. This Western Wall is now a place of pilgrimage and prayer.

## Beliefs

Judaism is a monotheistic religion. The core belief is contained in the declaration of faith, the *Shema*, which begins: "Hear, O Israel: the Lord our God, the Lord is one. And thou shalt love the Lord thy God with all thy heart, and with all thy soul, and with all thy might" (Deuteronomy 6:4–5).

God is an all-powerful, loving creator who has given Jews a particular spiritual calling to be his people. His name is holy and so many Jews will omit the vowel in writing G-d so as to preserve its sanctity.

## Scriptures

The Torah is the most sacred of Jewish texts. It contains the five books of Moses – Genesis, Exodus, Leviticus, Numbers, and Deuteronomy. These have stories of the patriarchs, including the giving of the Law to Moses, and the laws themselves. Torah scrolls are handwritten by a trained scribe who carefully copies each letter with a quill onto parchment. The text is in Hebrew and written from right to left. Readers use a pointer, a *yad*, so as not to touch the sacred text.

Some scholars argue that the Torah was woven together out of earlier documents and an oral tradition identified with different tribes in the region.

Some Jews, particularly Orthodox, take literally the account that God gave Moses the Torah in the desert. Whether they are taken literally or figuratively, these are the stories that have shaped Jewish life, and study of the Torah is highly prized.

The Tanakh, the wider Jewish Bible, contains histories, prophecy, wise sayings, and poetry covering a period to about 300 BC. It tells of David becoming the king, of Solomon building a temple, of many good and bad kings, and of foreigners occupying the land and the people going into exile.

### The Talmud

All modern Judaism stems from the formative period from around 100 BC to AD 500. The Rabbis (teachers) of this time set the pattern of interpreting the scriptures and how its laws could be applied to everyday life away from the Temple. After its fall in AD 70, when Temple sacrifices could no longer be observed, Rabbinic Judaism came to the ascendency. The Mishna and the Talmud are collections of the debates and teachings of these Rabbis. Modern interpretation takes account of what the Mishna and Talmud say before drawing conclusions. The Talmud refers to two collections, one known as the Palestinian (or Jerusalem) Talmud, the other the Babylonian Talmud. It contains both law (*halakah*) and lore/stories (*haggadah*).

## The State of Israel

By the beginning of the first millennium AD many Jews lived in communities around the Mediterranean with more joining them after the Romans quashed an uprising in AD 130. Over the next millennium Jewish communities became established through Eastern Europe (Ashkenazi Jews) and through North Africa to Spain (Sephardic Jews). There were periods of toleration and also times when Jews were persecuted and/or exiled. The phrase "next year in Jerusalem" became part of a prayer said at the festival of Passover.

Although some Jews did settle in Palestine over the centuries, a desire for the Promised Land was revived by the Zionist movement in the nineteenth century, and finally came to fruition with the establishment of the State of Israel in 1948, following the attempted genocide of the Jews by the Nazis in the Second World War. Modern memorial days remember the horror of the Holocaust and the founding of the State of Israel. All Jews have a right of return to Israel and many who live abroad holiday there. Some Orthodox Jews are opposed to the State of Israel. They believe that only the messiah can restore the state of Israel and he has not yet come.

There are over 13 million Jews worldwide, of whom over 5 million live in Israel.

## Branches of Orthodox Judaism

Haredi Judaism is a strict, ultra-orthodox branch of Judaism; its followers usually live in separate communities. Men devote themselves to the study of the Law. Haredi Jews are distinguished by their side curls and their dress, wearing black suits with white open-neck shirts and broad-brimmed hats – the style of central Europe, where the movement developed in the eighteenth century. There is also a glimpse of the fringe of their undergarment, a *tallit katan* ("little tallit"), an oblong cloth with a hole cut in it for the head. Each strand of the fringe stands for one of the laws. Women cover themselves completely, wearing thick tights even in the heat of Israel. Only their husbands may see their hair so they cover it with a wig or scarf.

The Kabbalah, followed by Hasidic and some other Jews, is the mystic tradition within Judaism, mainly developed in the medieval period but with earlier roots. It contemplates the soul's journey to God. Hasidic Jews, whose dress is similar to that of Haredi Jews, emphasize piety, joyful observance of the Commandments, and mysticism.

## Jewish ethics

Jewish teaching says all humanity is subject to the "code of Noah" (that is, the laws given by God to the "children of Noah"), which includes prohibition of murder and theft, but Jews should obey the 613 commandments, the *mitzvah*, found in the Torah. These begin with the Ten Commandments and extend to include practical laws for living in communities. The Rabbis extended these laws by applying them to new situations to ensure that the Law would not be broken by mistake, and rabbis today continue the long process of interpretation by applying the Law to a changing world in the light of earlier discussions. Where there is a conflict between saving a life and observation of a law (such as no travelling by car on the Sabbath), then saving a life takes precedence. The Law is a spiritual as well as an ethical path. It is through keeping the moral and ritual law that the follower becomes closer to God.

### The Ten Commandments

1. I am the Lord your God.
2. You shall have no other gods beside me. You shall not make a graven image.
3. You shall not take the name of the Lord your God in vain.
4. Remember the Sabbath day and keep it holy.

5. Honour your father and your mother.

6. You shall not murder.

7. You shall not commit adultery.

8. You shall not steal.

9. You shall not bear bear false witness.

10. You shall not covet your neighbour's wife.

Interpreting the 613 laws is one of the factors that divides modern Judaism, especially between the Orthodox – sometimes called Conservative – who follow literal observations of the Law, and the various Progressive and Reform movements that sprang up in the nineteenth century. These movements are more liberal in their interpretations of the scriptures and in giving equality to women. Some differences in interpretation (legal and cultural) also depend on whether the community is Ashkenazi (European) or Sephardic (North African and Spanish) in origin.

Summing up his view on the Law as laid out in the Torah, Rabbi Hillel, who taught in the first century BC, said, "What is hateful to you, do not do to your fellow man: this is the whole of the Law; the rest is mere commentary."

## Living the Jewish life

The family and a warm, hospitable home are at the heart of the Jewish faith, with rituals associated with festivals and family celebrations taking place in the home. Keeping the festivals together creates and maintains the community.

### Shabbat

*Shabbat*, or the Sabbath – the most important of all festivals because it is one of the Ten Commandments – takes place in the home. The house is cleaned, best clothes are worn, and food is prepared beforehand for this weekly celebration that lasts from before sunset on Friday to after sunset on Saturday. It begins when the mother lights the two Shabbat candles and ends with the separation ceremony of *havdalah*, which includes passing round a spice box symbolizing the hope that the sweet gifts of Shabbat will go into the week. No work will be done in that time and there is lots of merrymaking round the Friday evening meal.

Some Jews will not drive on Shabbat since all work is forbidden on that day, and the Mishnah lists lighting fires as a form of work. A car starts when the ignition is lit, so cars cannot be driven on Shabbat.

### Pesach

Observance of the spring festival of Pesach, or Passover, takes place in the home with a joyful family meal in which prayers, reading, rituals, and food entwine to retell the story of Moses leading the tribes out of Egypt and remind all participants that true freedom is found in serving God. Spring cleaning ensures that no leavened grain products from whisky to bread are left in the house. A place is laid for an unseen or unexpected guest, said to be the prophet Elijah.

## Sukkot

At the autumn festival of Sukkot an additional temporary room, built under an open sky, is often added to the house as the family recall their ancestors living in tents in the desert. The family eats in the Sukkah and some may sleep in it.

## Hanukkah

At Hanukkah, a December festival, an eight-branched candlestick is put in the window for the eight days of the festival as a sign that it is a Jewish home. The candles recall that it took eight days for fresh oil to arrive to light the candle in the Temple after the expulsion of the hated Seleucid conquerors in the second century BC from the land and from the Temple in Jerusalem.

## Time and food

Festivals shape the Jewish year. Each one has its own food, making it distinctive:

- The Shabbat includes two sweet *challah,* fresh bread rolls that recall the bread God provided in the desert.

- For Rosh Hashanah (New Year), celebrants eat apples dipped in honey, wishing sweetness for the year.

- At Sukkot an etrog, a lemon-like fruit, is bound with willow, palm, and myrtle to wave during the festival.

- Hanukkah is known for doughnuts and potato latkes – food made with oil – remembering the oil in the lamp that was lit again at the rededication of the Temple.

- At Passover bread and cakes are all unleavened to recall that there was no time for the bread to rise when the people left Egypt. The *seder* (meaning order) table is also set with a plate containing symbols of Jewish history.

### Keeping a kosher home

Observant Jews try to keep a home where food is kosher – fit for consumption according to Jewish law.

No pork is allowed, certain sea foods are prohibited, and animals must be killed according to ritual. Milk and meat products must not be consumed together and are kept separately. Food is passed as kosher by the Beth Din, a rabbinical court.

Jewish homes, synagogues, and offices usually have small oblong boxes nailed to every doorpost except the toilet. These are *mezuzahs* containing the words of the *Shema* on a tiny scroll, following the instruction in Deuteronomy to nail the words to the doorpost. A short ceremony is held when a new *mezuzah* is installed.

Blessings are said as part of rituals and incidentally through the day – they are for the good things in life, for example, children, a meal, grapes, wine, the new day, and the new moon.

### Daily prayer

There are three set times for reciting prayers, which have themes of repentance, hope of the messiah, and blessings. At morning prayers, a prayer shawl (*tallit*) is worn and two small boxes (*tefillin*) containing the words of the *Shema* are worn. A leather strap is used to bind one *tefellin* round the head. Another strap is wound round the left arm and between the fingers to bind the *tefillin* near the heart. The binding of the *tefellin* is in obedience to the biblical command found in Deuteronomy 11:18–20.

## Synagogue

Jewish communal life is based on the synagogue. It
is a place for prayer, study, social gatherings, and the
organization of welfare. Some communities call their
place of worship temple or *shul* (school). Praying
together is valued and some Jews will try to attend
the synagogue daily to make up a *minyan*, the ten
individuals required for prayer. The main service is on
Shabbat.

A cantor leads the congregation in singing
services. He may also be the rabbi, the community's
teacher. Synagogues are independent, each one
employing its own rabbi who often will have studied
at a *yeshiva*, a college, in Israel.

Synagogues always have an ark, or cupboard,
usually on the east wall to face Jerusalem. It houses
the Torah scrolls, furled inside ornate covers. A
Torah scroll is processed to a flat desk, a *bimah*, for
reading. At Simchat Torah the Torah scrolls are held
high and danced round the synagogue to cheering.
It marks the end of the annual cycle of reading from
the Torah. Synagogues also have a lamp hanging from
the ceiling to symbolize the eternal light of God. They
often have the Ten Commandments displayed.

At Rosh Hashanah, New Year, congregations gather
to hear the blowing of the *shofar*, a ram's horn, the call
for repentance. Synagogues are also full ten days later
for the services on the holy and solemn day of Yom
Kippur, a twenty-five hour fast for atonement of sins.

There are no images of living creatures in synagogues because the second of the Ten Commandments prohibits making images.

## Rites of passage

Boys are circumcised on the eighth day after birth by a man trained for the task, a *mohel*. This is to follow a command given to Abraham. The ceremony often takes place at home. Boys and girls are usually given a Hebrew name, though they may have a secular one as well.

At thirteen a boy is old enough to read the Torah scroll at synagogue services and be counted as part of the *minyan*. He has become a *Bar Mitzvah*, a "son of the commandment". He usually prepares thoroughly for his first reading at the synagogue, and this is often an occasion for a family party.

Marriage is traditionally for companionship and procreation. To marry is holy and the fulfilment of a commandment. There is a tradition that there is a *beshert* – a soulmate for each person. A *ketubah*, a contract of obligations between groom and bride, is drawn up before the wedding and signed in front of witnesses. The many customs associated with weddings recall the stories of the marriages of the Patriarchs – Abraham, Isaac, and Jacob. Some of the ceremony – the readings and blessing – takes place under a *chuppah*, a decorated canopy open on all sides and symbolizing the Jewish home that welcomes all. At the end of the ceremony the groom smashes a glass under his foot. This is said to symbolize the destruction of the Temple in Jerusalem.

### Men and women

In the Orthodox traditions, many of the rituals and the role of rabbi are confined to men only. Men and women also sit separately. Many Jewish men and boys wear a small cap called a *kippa* or *yarmulka* to show their Jewish identity and, some say, to indicate they are lower than God. Many of the denominations in the Reform, or Progressive, movements have *Bat Mizvah* ceremonies for girls at the age of twelve – they are "daughters of the commandment". In the more liberal traditions women sometimes wear prayer shawls and may be rabbis.

### *Death and burial*

Rites associated with death are concerned with giving dignity to the deceased, who is never left unguarded, and comforting the bereaved. Bodies are buried facing Jerusalem as soon as possible in a simple shroud without a coffin. Sons have a duty to say the *Kaddish* prayer in a *minyan* for eleven months and on the anniversary of the death. This prayer blesses God and longs for his kingdom. There is a general belief in an afterlife where suffering will be vindicated and the good rewarded.

# Shinto

Shinto is the ancient indigenous religion of Japan. It means "Way of the *kami*". *Kami* are awe-inspiring mysterious powers that are sometimes described as spirits or deities. They are found in natural places, in waterfalls and mountains, in certain trees, rocks, or unusual features in the landscape. Some *kami* are divine beings linked to creation, some are founding figures of a village or patrons of a particular trade, and others reside in the home or in sacred objects.

The interaction between the spiritual and material worlds is central to Shinto as the *kami* influence everyday life. Japanese live the way of the *kami* and maintain continuity and harmony through prayer and ritual, passing on Shinto values and traditions from generation to generation.

Pilgrimage is a way to connect with the *kami* of nature, to experience the power and beauty of sacred sites and seek blessings of the *kami*. Shrines to resident *kami* are dotted along the slopes of Mount Fuji, or *Fujisan*, a volcano that last erupted in 1707 and Japan's highest mountain. This peak is venerated as the home of the goddess Konohana-sakuya-hime – the princess who makes the trees blossom.

## Beginnings

The divine origins of Japan and its history are told in two books: *The Record of Ancient Matters* (AD 712) and *The Chronicles of Japan* (AD 720). They record the beliefs and traditions of Shinto and account for the succession of emperors, including the descent of the imperial family from the sun goddess, Amaterasu.

In Shinto the universe has always existed. At first it was a formless mass that divided to form the heavens and the earth. An original deity appeared, followed by a divine couple, and gradually the heavenly *kami* were born. One couple, a brother and sister called Izangi and Izanami, were sent to earth. In turn, they gave birth to the islands, elements, land, and waters of Japan. Their children flourished and the ancestors of the Japanese people were created.

## Body of the *kami*

*Shintai*, or "body of the *kami*", are objects where the *kami* reside – this could be a mirror, sword, jewel, or natural feature. Shrines are built to house *shintai*, which are wrapped in clothes, placed in a box, and kept in a sanctuary at the heart of a shrine.

A *shintai* is ceremoniously removed and installed in a portable shrine at *matsuri* (festivals), when it is processed through the streets to bestow blessings on the local area and its inhabitants. Thousands of people gather for these *matsuri*, although the *shintai* itself is never on public view during the procession or when it is resident in the shrine.

## Shinto ritual

Purification is an important part of Shinto ritual, and visitors will wash their hands and cleanse their mouths with clear running water before entering a shrine. Worshippers sometimes leave offerings such as money, food, or rice cakes, and write requests to the *kami* on slips of white paper that are then tied to a sacred sakaki tree.

There is a strong sense of family and community affiliation within Shinto, and children learn its traditions and rituals from an early age. When asked, many Japanese will say they follow both Shinto and Buddhism, and different temples are used for different rites. For example, a couple may marry at a Shinto temple or celebrate Shinto festivals, but offer personal devotion at a Buddhist temple.

# Sikhism

The Sikh way of life is one spent meditating on God, Waheguru, "the great teacher", and following God's will in serving others. *Sikh* means "disciple". God is known through meditation on his word and the wonders of creation. Reincarnation follows death but leads ultimately to the soul reuniting with God.

Ninety per cent of the world's 24 million Sikhs live in the Punjab, India, and there are growing communities elsewhere in the world, including North America, the UK, and Australia.

## Beginnings

Sikhism began in fifteenth-century India with the teachings of Guru Nanak, a young Hindu who lived in the Punjab area of India, then ruled by Muslims. He preached against the quarreling between Hindus and Muslims, teaching that God was neither Hindu nor Muslim but Waheguru, the one God. He was critical of those who performed rituals without meaning. He taught the equality of all people regardless of their birth and travelled extensively with a companion, Mardana, singing hymns, before establishing a community based on equality.

## Equality of all

In the next 200 years Sikhism developed under the leadership of a further nine Gurus. During this time a lake and temple – the *Harimandir*, or House of God – were built at Amritsar in the Punjab. The House of God at Amritsar was built to house the first collection of hymns. It is sometimes called "the Golden Temple" as it is covered in gold leaf. The temple has doors opening in the four directions to welcome people from all over the world. This site continues to be a place of pilgrimage and a focal point for the Sikh community.

By the time of Guru Gobind Singh in the seventeenth century, the Sikhs had become a fighting force standing against religious discrimination and injustice and working for the poor and the needy. Several Sikh gurus were killed in battle or martyred. The ninth guru, Tegh Bahadur, is remembered for defending the rights of Hindus on the principle of religious freedom for all.

The last living guru, Guru Gobind Singh, named the Sikh scriptures as the final guru for all time. These scriptures, the Guru Granth Sahib, would be his successor to guide the Sikh community, the *Panth*.

**The Sikh flag**
The swords on the Sikh flag have multiple meanings. One is that the temporal and spiritual worlds are bound together; another is the willingness to promote justice.

## Khalsa: Sikh brotherhood

Guru Gobind Singh inaugurated the Khalsa, a brotherhood of Sikhs, in 1699. He also gave them five symbols to signify their commitment:

- *Kesh* – uncut hair
- *Kara* – a steel bracelet, symbolizing that God who is truth has no beginning or end
- *Kanga* – a wooden comb keeping the hair neat and tidy
- *Kacchera* – a type of short trousers worn by horsemen
- *Kirpan* – a sword.

Sikh men wear turbans to keep their hair tidy and to identify with the gurus.

The first members of the Khalsa were the *Panj Pyare*, the five holy ones, who demonstrated their courage and commitment by being willing to be sacrificed for their faith. This is recalled at the festival of Baisakhi on

13 April, or on the first day of the month of Vaisakh in the Nanakshahi calendar, which counts from the birth of Guru Nanak in 1469.

The Sikh surnames of "Singh" for men, meaning lion, and "Kaur" for women, meaning princess, were given by Guru Gobind Singh as a sign of equality in contrast to the caste system where names signified status.

## The Sikh scriptures

The Guru Granth Sahib is a collection of hymns written mainly by the Sikh gurus but also includes hymns by Hindu and Muslim saints. *Guru* means "one who leads to light", *Granth* means "writings", and *Sahib* means Lord. The Guru Granth Sahib is believed to be God's living word, and it guides all aspects of life. The five daily prayers are taken from it. Its hymns are sung during Sikh worship at the *gurdwara*, parents use it in choosing their babies' names, the bride and groom walk round it during the wedding service, and important decisions are made in its presence. It is read at death and during the cremation services when the soul is released. The scriptures are read in their entirety at the festivals – this takes around forty-eight hours.

### The gurdwara

*Gurdwara* means "House of the Guru". The Guru Granth Sahib always has a room of its own at the *gurdwara*. It is laid on ornate cushions and held high above the head when it is processed between its room to a decorated platform in the prayer hall. It is always treated with great respect. Anyone, man or woman, who reads the Guru Granth Sahib can be called *granthi*. However, many *gurdwaras* have someone in a ministering role who is also known as the *granthi*.

A sweet food called *karah parshad* is shared among the congregation at the end of the service. This has been blessed by ceremoniously stirring it with the point of a *kirpan*.

Every *gurdwara* has a *langar*, free kitchen, embodying the Sikh ideals of equality and service to the community. The food is vegetarian and all can eat there whatever their religious background or status. Other Sikh values include forgiveness, charity, honesty, striving for justice, and self-sacrifice.

# Zoroastrianism

Zoroastrianism is described in its scriptures as the "good religion". Zoroastrians believe in a cosmic struggle between good and evil, between the spirit of the eternal God and the destructive spirit. Moral actions, truthful behaviour, and religious ritual help outweigh the negative consequences of hatred, greed, and violence. To strengthen the forces of good, Zoroastrians try to work actively in the community at large.

The sacred texts of Zoroastrianism are called the Avesta. They were handed down orally before being recorded in Iran in the fifth to sixth centuries AD using a specially invented alphabet. The language of the texts is called Avestan.

The Zoroastrians who left Iran (Persia) over a thousand years ago in search of religious freedom and settled in India were called Parsis (after the country of their origin). The majority of Zoroastrians still live in India, but there are communities in other countries including Iran, the UK, USA, Canada, Singapore, Australia, and New Zealand.

## Beginnings

Zoroastrianism arose from the teachings of Zoroaster
who lived between 1400 and 1200 BC in north-
east Iran. Born into a priestly class at a time when
his people were subject to warfare and injustice,
Zoroaster meditated upon the nature of good and evil
and experienced a series of divine revelations. He
preached that there was one just and transcendent
God, Ahura Mazda, or "Wise Lord", who created all
that is good. But there are two primal spirits in conflict
with each other in this world. One is order and truth
– this is Ahura Mazda in the form of the Holy Spirit,
Spenta Mainyu. The other is chaos and destruction in
the form of Angra Mainyu.

Zoroaster recorded his beliefs and his vision for
this new faith in seventeen hymns called the "Gathas",
which are part of the Avesta. Verses from these hymns
are included in daily prayers that are said five times a
day. Zoroastrians bathe to ritually purify themselves
before prayer, rituals, or ceremonies.

### Free will

Zoroastrians believe that God gave people free will
to choose truth and goodness over evil. Each person
has a *fravashi*, a guardian spirit containing the divine
and incorruptible essence of Ahura Mazda. *Fravashis*
guide individuals through life, helping them live with
integrity in thought, word, and deed.

## Sacred fire

Fire is the sacred symbol of Ahura Mazda, and every Zoroastrian temple has a fire room at its centre. Specially consecrated fires, lit by wood, are tended by priests and never extinguished, although there is a type of sacred fire that can be tended by lay people. All rituals and ceremonies are carried out in the presence of fire.

## Holy days

Tradition says Zoroaster established the seven obligatory holy days to celebrate Ahura Mazda and his creations. New Year, or *No Ruz*, is the greatest of these – the day when fire, the seventh creation, is celebrated. It is a festival of prayer and family celebration that looks forward to the renewal of the world – the final triumph of good over evil following a mighty battle. The dead will then be resurrected and united with their *fravashi* (guardian spirit), and the saved will live eternally in Ahura Mazda's perfect kingdom.